PROTECTION
SPELLS

CLEAR NEGATIVE ENERGY, BANISH UNHEALTHY INFLUENCES, AND EMBRACE YOUR POWER

ARIN MURPHY-HISCOCK
Author of *The Green Witch*

ADAMS MEDIA

NEW YORK   LONDON   TORONTO   SYDNEY   NEW DELHI

Adams Media
An Imprint of Simon & Schuster, Inc.
57 Littlefield Street
Avon, Massachusetts 02322

First Adams Media hardcover edition August 2018

ADAMS MEDIA and colophon are trademarks of Simon & Schuster.

For information about special discounts for bulk purchases, please contact Simon & Schuster Special Sales at 1-866-506-1949 or business@simonandschuster.com.

The Simon & Schuster Speakers Bureau can bring authors to your live event. For more information or to book an event contact the Simon & Schuster Speakers Bureau at 1-866-248-3049 or visit our website at www.simonspeakers.com.

Interior design by Katrina Machado
Interior images © Getty Images/Adobest, Hollygraphic, ryccio, JuliarStudio, PandaVector

Manufactured in the United States of America

10 9 8 7 6

Library of Congress Cataloging-in-Publication Data has been applied for.

ISBN 978-1-5072-0832-8
ISBN 978-1-5072-0833-5 (ebook)

This one is for the Liberal Stitches, who defend, protect, and fight for what's right. Thank you for being the excellent women you are and for being there to support and celebrate me when I need it. Although the Coven of Let's Hang Out Sometime is spread across several continents, you are always close to my heart.

CONTENTS

INTRODUCTION

Whether you are seeking to protect your emotional well-being, reinforce your confidence, or find some comfort in a stressful world, protection spells can help. Feeling unsafe puts a strain on your emotional state and robs you of energy, but the spells in this book can strengthen your comfort and security and heal your body and mind.

Spellcrafting can help you feel more secure, protect your positive energy, and bring the kind of comfort that allows you to relax and live your life to its full potential. It can also help you extend the same to your family, friends, and possessions.

If taking charge of defending yourself, both your energy and your physical body, interests you, then spellcrafting can help. If you've never done spellwork before, don't worry; *Protection Spells* is designed to introduce you to the concept and the practice. Many of these spells don't require anything other than you yourself and a bit of creative visualization. You don't need to be an established, experienced practitioner of spellcraft in order to use this book! The spells are simple, and the book is designed to give you the knowledge and tools you need to put together a simple spell of your own. For example:

- Part 1 looks at spellcrafting in the modern world. It explores what a spell is, how spells work, and some of the basics surrounding spellcraft that are useful to know when starting out.

- Part 2 is a collection of spells focusing on defense and protection divided into various categories. They're designed to be quick, relatively easy to perform, and accessible to as many people as possible.

- Part 3 provides three full-length protection rituals for you to explore: one for protecting a home, one for protecting an object, and one for protecting a person. You'll also find sections for ingredients or components you might want to draw on in creating your own protection spells, such as crystals and stones, herbs, and symbology, as well as different ways in which these can be used.

Protection Spells is at its heart a quick reference guide to doing protection and defensive magic. There are a lot of ready-made spells available in its pages, but my true hope is that you'll take these spells and use them as the basis for your own spells, created by you with your own goals, your own associations, and your own supplies and ingredients. With your own life and those of your loved ones well protected with your spells, you can live with more freedom, comfort, and joy. So let's get started!

PART 1:
SPELLCRAFTING

CHAPTER 1:
AN INTRODUCTION TO SPELLCRAFTING

What is spellcraft? It's the art of using energy to help regulate your world, to attune yourself to the energies around you, and to work with those energies for a beneficial outcome. It's important to note that a spell is *not* a religious act. Rather, spellcrafting is a method of using energy to power some sort of change. Using spells to protect and defend yourself, the people you care about, and various areas of your life can be part of supporting healthy living. Working protection magic can help reduce the amount of stress you have to deal with on a daily basis, and magical maintenance of your energy can help your emotional and physical well-being. Spellcraft can assist you with all this and more.

WHAT IS A SPELL?

A spell is something you do with intent and awareness to create change on some level, and works on the principle that everything is connected by energy. Spells are done by performing a sequence of symbolic actions in the physical world to activate change on a different level. A spell looks to affect a situation by introducing a new kind of energy or by redistributing the energy that is already present.

When casting a spell, you function as an agent of change; you actively call upon resources to gather and direct energy. When you cast a spell, you acknowledge that your actions are the ones responsible for creating change. Initializing change is your intention, and whatever consequences follow are also your responsibility. (More on that in the sections on ethics.)

CAUTION: WORK AHEAD

Spellwork is designed to make your life easier. However, if you're looking to use spells to avoid work, you are in for a rude awakening. Spellcraft requires effort, thought, energy, and focus. You can't snap your fingers and expect instant change to check off whatever goals you're working toward. Spellcraft is a transformative process that touches you as the spellcaster as well as your goals and the environment that contains them. Energy and effort on your part must be put into the equation in order for the outcome to manifest. So you still have to do work in order to achieve your goal, but you're more in control of what happens and how.

HOW DO SPELLS WORK?

Everything in the world possesses energy of some kind, including situations. All those energies reach out to connect with one another, creating a weblike connection. When you seek to influence a situation with a spell, you tweak the energy in one location. That tweak sends shivers all through the web, and every energy field ripples a bit as your spell's energy travels to the point it seeks to modify. The world is covered with these strands of energy connecting everyone and everything, and this is what enables you to send out certain energies toward a goal or pull certain energies toward you.

YOU ARE THE MOST IMPORTANT PART OF A SPELL

What makes a spell go? What differentiates spells from chemistry and cooking is the inclusion of *you*, your *will*, and your *intention*. You are an agent of change. Your action stimulates the energy. Your will determines the movement of the energy. Your intention directs it to execute the changes you wish to see.

Does it work immediately? No. What you need to do once you've cast a spell is be confident that the transformation you desire has already begun and will resolve soon. Then watch for and be aware of change. When that change may come is variable. It may creep in bit by bit until one day something's different, and you're not quite sure when it started; it's just the new normal. Rarely are changes staggeringly obvious and dramatic.

PROTECTION MAGIC

After a decade or so of quiet, there's a resurgence of interest in the metaphysical these days. With an increasing load of stress deriving from the ongoing barrage of news and information coming at them every minute, people look for ways to set their minds at rest and feel like they have a hand in protecting and defending what they consider good and right in the world. Protection magic is one way for you to do that.

DEFENSE AGAINST THE DARK ARTS?

As dramatic as defending yourself against monsters and dark magic sounds, you actually don't run into a lot of it on a daily basis. It is extremely rare that someone will actively use aggressive magic aimed at you or engage in deliberate psychic attack.

However, there *is* a bunch of negative energy out there in the world. Hatred, fear, anger—it's inescapable. And if you're sensitive to energy, it can really affect you. It can go so far as to adversely impact your physical health, making you ill. Even if you're not sensitive to energy, it can affect you, sapping your energy so you're tired, snappish, and generally exhausted for no clear reason.

Protection has several facets to it. You can protect something from general negativity. You can protect something or someone from a specific danger. You can defend against an attack, deliberate or environmental. You can protect someone, somewhere, or something from negativity by maintaining a field of positive energy around it. And perhaps most importantly, you can maintain a level of defense at all times because prevention is the best medicine.

WHEN DO YOU NEED PROTECTION?

Everyone could use more protection; safety is so important. But there are times when you feel particularly vulnerable and may want to increase your defenses.

Are you experiencing what feels like a run of bad luck? Are you becoming overwhelmed by sensations or discomfort that you can't clearly identify, or are you having particularly vivid or disturbing dreams? These can all be signs that there's negativity cluttering up your personal energy or the spaces in which you operate.

It's also not uncommon to start being more aware of different energies as you start to work with spells. After all, spellwork is about working with energy, and the more you do it, the better you get at sensing, reading, and moving energy. Your new awareness can make you feel like your senses are set to maximum reception, and it can be overwhelming. Don't assume you're under some sort of attack; you're just sorting through all the new information you're picking up.

Here are some techniques to help you acclimate to this new sensitivity of awareness:

- Practice centering and grounding (see Chapter 2).

- Spend some time outdoors.

- Engage in physical activity to help you focus on your body to balance out the new energy awareness.

- Take care of yourself. Eat right, drink enough water, get enough sleep, meditate.

- Journal. Write down everything you're experiencing and keep track of the spellwork you're doing to see if there's any sort of correlation.

- Do regular magical rituals to cleanse yourself and your living space to reduce the amount of energy interference.

- Be patient with yourself and the process.

BE AWARE

Spellcraft affects the person doing it, just as it affects whatever he or she is casting at. Working with spells gives you a heightened sense of energy and awareness that boosts your everyday alertness.

Sometimes spellwork is just a heightened awareness of potential danger; that mindfulness allows you to tap into the energy of your environment and pay attention so you notice problems before they become significant. This is key in protection: becoming aware of a problem before it becomes a problem, while it's still in the developmental stage. It's easier to deal with a developing problem than one that has grown into a massive issue.

Your best defense in your day-to-day life is to be aware of situations, your environment, and people's energies. Heightened awareness can alert you to a potentially bad situation before it actually starts so you can get out or invoke major protection before the negative energy comes down.

INTUITION

Sometimes you just get an odd feeling, as if something's not quite right. Or perhaps you feel prompted to go a different way to work for no reason that you can clearly point to. That's your intuition at work.

Intuition is an instinctive prompting that arises from your mind or body picking up information that you may not be consciously aware of. Remember that web of energy mentioned earlier? Energy carries information, which is how you can use spells to affect a situation elsewhere. The reverse is also true: information in the form of energy can come to you as well. Your conscious mind is usually taken up with focusing on a zillion other things, so reading this energy is often left to your subconscious.

Trust your intuition. It can help keep you safe. It's another level of awareness that can benefit by association when you work with spells. Remember, a lot of protection is rooted in prevention. Listening to and trusting your intuition can help you avoid situations in which your safety might be threatened.

ETHICS

One of the most critical elements to take into account during spellcraft is ethics—specifically the ethics of whom your magic focuses on. In general, the person to affect is *you*. You are the person you have the most control over. You are also the person for whom you have given yourself permission to do magic.

If you are doing spellwork to improve a situation that involves a problematic individual, you work to change the *situation*, not the person. What about using magic to enhance the protection of your spouse who works in a dangerous job? Again, you could work to improve the situation, but what if you specifically want to protect the *person*?

You don't get to do magic on or for other people without their permission. Ask! It's a simple matter of respect. You wouldn't walk up to someone and suit them up in plate armor or hockey gear without asking first, right? Same goes for magic. If you're feeling awkward, a simple, "Hey, I'm worried about you in [specific situation]. Do you mind if I do a little something spiritually to help keep you safe?" If they're open, you could even discuss a method. Would they like a charged stone to carry with them, for example?

What do you do if they say no? You can elaborate; they may need a clearer explanation in order to understand what you're proposing. If they still say no, you have a very difficult decision to make. You can either comply with their wishes…or go ahead with your magic.

This is a huge issue, and not a decision to be taken lightly. If you opt to do magic on or for someone who has not agreed to it, then you accept responsibility not only for any outcome of that magic, but also for your decision to work against your friend's wishes. That's a heavy karmic burden.

You must weigh the situation very, very carefully. Are you afraid for your friend's life? Is the situation serious enough to merit you proceeding anyway? If not, then you probably have no business doing it.

TRY ANOTHER APPROACH

Instead of doing magic on one specific individual, use a blanket spell that doesn't necessarily focus on one individual but protects all your friends and family. Or work on yourself: do a spell to help you be the best friend you can be to support those in need.

What if you're doing spellwork on an area, such as a room? Area magic can be an ethically gray area. If it's your room, you're fine. Whoever walks through it will interact with it on a personal level, but since the magic isn't specifically aimed at them, you should be okay. What if you need or want to do magic on a common area, like a conference room at work? First of all, examine your motivation carefully. Doing spellwork to influence people in a meeting to support you is not cool. Instead, charge and carry a stone to increase your likeability, improve your communication skills, and help you deliver your arguments clearly. That way, you're working on yourself; you're the target or subject. Alternatively, you may want to cast an area spell for positivity and efficiency to help the meeting run smoothly and in a focused manner. Again, you're not performing magic on individuals without their permission; you're inviting universally beneficial, supportive energy into the space.

EXCEPTIONS

There are exceptions to this ethical rule: your kids and pets. Even then, there are still ethical aspects to consider. As a parent, you are the responsible legal guardian for your children. You make the decisions regarding how to keep them safe and how to care for them. That said, it's polite and respectful to ask their permission if they're old enough. Better yet, work protection magic together!

SPELLCASTING WITH KIDS

It's interesting to design new spells with children; they come up with fascinating parallels and connections that work very well for them. A lot of the spells in this book can be adapted for kids. The key is to simplify! For kid-focused spells, see Chapter 4.

What about pets? As with your kids, you are the person legally responsible for your animals, and you make decisions regarding their safety and care. They are sentient beings, however, and you can ask them if they are open to magic. You might receive the impression that they're fine with it. If they seem uncomfortable or clearly against the idea, you can choose to respect their wishes or go ahead if you deem it the best course of action.

SPELLCRAFT PRIMER

There are some basic things to know before you start casting spells. This section will examine workspaces and environments, planned versus spontaneous spellcasting, protecting yourself (do you need a circle or not?), and other associated things.

WHAT'S A CIRCLE, AND DO YOU NEED ONE?

In magical work, a circle serves as a container for keeping the energy sympathetic to your goal inside and other energies outside. The circle also serves a mental function for you. By taking the time to create a circle, you are emphasizing in your mind that your working area is being set apart from everyday life. Inside the circle, you and your spell connect the current reality with your desired reality. A circle can help you focus on your goal and bring you closer to it.

When should you cast a circle? Ask yourself the following questions:

- Am I in an unfamiliar place?
- Am I likely to be distracted?
- Is my spell complicated?
- Is my spell going to take a long time?

If you answer yes to two or more of these questions, it's probably a good idea to create a circle before you cast your spell.

BASIC CIRCLE CAST

In some spiritual paths, a circle sets apart a sacred space in which to do devotional worship. However, a circle is also an energy container, keeping what you're focusing on clear of distraction or interference from unwanted energy. This second point is why using a circle in spellcraft can be beneficial.

CIRCLE PROTECTION

A basic circle can also be a protective shield for yourself, an item, an object, or a space. See Part 2 for spells using this concept.

If it helps you, you can make a physical circle around your chosen space with a long cord or set a line of objects such as shells or rocks around you. Different people like different-sized circles; if you're alone and not planning on moving around very much, a circle approximately 6 feet in diameter should be fine. Hold your arms out to the sides, fingers extended, to get a sense of how wide your basic circle can be. Plan to create your energy barrier slightly beyond your reach if it makes you more comfortable. If you're going to be moving around the room, try casting the circle right to the walls.

Building this circle uses the energies of the four cardinal directions and their associated elements. It asks that you envision the four classical elements—earth, water, air, and fire—but if you like, you can also have physical representations of them in the form of a stone, a small dish of water, a feather or incense, and a small candle with you. Place each at the associated cardinal point—the stone for north, the feather or incense for east, the candle for south, the water for west—or set them up at your workspace.

ELEMENTAL REPRESENTATIONS

If you want all four elements represented in your circle but only want a minimal number of items, put a pinch of salt in a small dish of water for earth and water, and use a lighted stick or cone of incense to represent both air and fire.

Basic Circle Cast

Before you begin, use a compass or a compass app on your phone to determine which way is north.

1. Center and ground (see Chapter 2).
2. Stand facing east. Say, *"Energies of the east, of new light and stirring air, I call upon you to help create my circle of protection."*

3. Turn to the south, imagining a line of energy traveling from the east to the south. Face the south and say, *"Energies of the south, of passion and bright flame, I call upon you to help create my circle of protection."*

4. Turn to the west, imagining a line of energy traveling from the south to the west. Face west and say, *"Energies of the west, of transformation and flowing water, I call upon you to help create my circle of protection."*

5. Turn to the north, imagining the line of energy continuing from the west to the north. Face north and say, *"Energies of the north, of stability and rich earth, I call upon you to help create my circle of protection."*

6. Turn to the east again, imagining the line of energy traveling from the north to meet the beginning of the line, forming a complete circle. Visualize the energy growing upward from that line encircling you to meet above you in a dome, then imagine the same thing happening beneath you until you are surrounded by a sphere of energy.

7. Say, *"The circle is cast; by the powers of earth, air, fire, and water, I am protected."*

8. Once your circle is cast, you can go ahead and do whatever you need to do: spellwork, meditation, anything.

9. When you are done, stand in the center of your sphere again and raise your hands above your head. Slowly lower them, visualizing the energy dome above you opening and lowering down to the line again. Visualize the half sphere beneath you melting away likewise. Say, *"Earth, air, fire, water, thank you for your protection and your help today."*

Can't have an open flame where you're working? Use something else that represents fire, like a photo, a drawing, or a small LED candle.

What do you do if you have to cross the circle for some reason during the spell? Take a moment to imagine an archway growing in the energy wall of the circle, through which you can step for a moment. When you return, imagine the archway shrinking away until all that's left is the smooth unmarred energy wall again. Note that this isn't ideal for extended absences; if you have a two-part spell where the second part doesn't immediately follow the first, do the first part, take down the circle, then cast a new circle for the second part at a later time.

WORKING WITHOUT A CIRCLE

You won't always have the time or opportunity to create a circle before you do spellwork; sometimes you need to act immediately in a dangerous or time-sensitive situation. Other times, when you're in a safe, familiar place, you won't need to set up any kind of defense or protection. In situations such as this, or when you don't feel that you need a full-blown circle, you can invoke protection for your work by saying something like this short charm:

World above, world below,
Energy come, energy flow,
Protective light circles round me,
Mountains and sky, flame and sea.

An alternate method is simply to visualize a circle of light around you.

WHAT'S AN ALTAR, AND DO YOU NEED ONE?

An altar is just a dedicated workspace. In a religious context, it's used during worship. In this book, the spells are designed to be performed anywhere; you don't need a blessed, dedicated space to work magic.

That said, if you do want a dedicated workspace, go ahead and make a little shelf or space on a side table on which to set out your magical working. Some people like to have a dedicated cloth that can be spread out to make a workspace wherever they like.

The key is to be comfortable. Some people like to have a magical frame of mind triggered by working in the same place each time, in the same surroundings. They may go so far as to wear the same clothing or burn the same incense. Experiment and find out what works for you.

CASTING

Here are some basic things to remember while casting:

- It's important to perform each action with intent and visualize your goal while you're doing it. This reinforces the energy you're pulling together and codes it for your specific goal. Remember, spells don't work because you put together two herbs and a stone; they work because you're using those objects associated with your goal to help energize your will and intention.

- Make sure you have all your necessary supplies with you before you begin. Nothing derails magic and focus like having to get up and go fetch a lighter or a pair of scissors in the middle of a spell. If that happens, just stop and start all over again a bit later.

- Turn off your phone and close your door to minimize distraction. If there's ambient noise that you can't shut out, try putting on headphones and listening to soft music that gets you into the headspace you need to be in for whatever spellwork you're doing.

- Decide if you need a defined circle or if you can work your spell without one.

TYPES OF SPELLS

In this book you'll encounter a variety of spellwork styles. Here's a brief overview of the different methods you'll encounter so you'll be familiar with them as they show up.

AMULETS

An amulet is a passive object that you carry or wear that extends its power to you to ward or protect you. If you feel uncomfortable or exposed when you aren't wearing a favorite bracelet, necklace, pendant, or ring, that piece of jewelry is already a sort of amulet: it defines part of your energy, and you associate it with your sense of self.

The previous example is an amulet that has evolved into being simply by virtue of the fact that you're carrying it or wearing it often and it has become a part of you. When consciously creating an amulet, you can make choices based on the object's symbol or traditional associations, your personal associations with it, the shape and color, and the material from which it's made.

CHARM BAGS

Charm bags are small pouches of objects or ingredients gathered and charged for a purpose. These are also called talisman bags, gris-gris bags, conjure bags, and mojo bags, among other names. A Native American medicine pouch serves a similar purpose. A variety of objects are carried in the pouch; these reflect the individual's own personal medicine or energy, or serve to redress an imbalance or weakness in his or her energy at that time.

A charm bag can either be a general thing, designed to support your energy overall, or tailored to a specific use, such as good health, defense from bad luck, and so forth. Unlike an amulet, which wards, charm bags and talismans actively draw things toward you.

CORD AND KNOT MAGIC

Once upon a time, sailors carried knotted cords that witches had made for them. To summon wind when they needed it, they would untie a knot, releasing the magic held within. Knots are a great way to do magic in advance and hold it ready to be released when it's needed. Knots can also bind something, keeping it from roaming free and harming others.

Cotton, silk, wool, and linen are ideal fibers to use. Try to avoid nylon and acrylic. The material you use doesn't have to be cord at all, of course; you can do knot spells with yarn, embroidery floss, tapestry wool, and strips of material. Any kind of crafting with string can be classified as cord magic, so if you knit, crochet, needlepoint, or weave, you can apply those skills to cord magic.

CANDLE MAGIC

Candle magic is one of the most popular types of spellcraft out there, and it's no wonder. Candles are easy to get and easy to use. Candle magic is very flexible, adapting to your needs. As a candle burns down, you can imagine an obstacle melting away or imagine the energy you've imbued it with being released to do its work. Alternatively, you can see it as your goal being drawn toward you as the wax melts away.

Any kind of candle can be used. Tea lights and birthday candles are ideal, as they burn quickly. Take a new candle that hasn't previously been used for a specific purpose, hold it in your hands, think very hard about your desire or need, then light it. Make sure you have a clearly defined goal or outcome in mind; don't think in circles around the issue. The more clearly you visualize the goal, the more effective it will be. For added support, choose a candle color you associate with the positive outcome of the spell. (See Chapter 7 for a reference list of colors and their associated energies.)

CHARGING AND EMPOWERING

Charging and *empowering* refer to programming an object or ingredient for your spell. Essentially, it means taking your clearly defined goal and imprinting it into the item, using your personal energy directed by your willpower. In the candle magic example, you are empowering the candle with your need or command.

SYMPATHETIC MAGIC

Sympathetic magic isn't a technique so much as a classification. Sympathetic magic dictates that whatever happens to a thing representing someone or something else will also happen to the thing or person being represented. A voodoo doll is a classic example of sympathetic magic. It's also referred to as imitative magic and is based on the idea of correspondence between the situation being represented and the representation itself. In protection spells, the thing or person you're working to protect will be the subject of your representation.

CONTAGIOUS MAGIC

Contagious magic is another classification. Contagious magic is exemplified by someone or something touching a charged or enchanted object in order to absorb its qualities. It also works the other way; anything that was in contact with a person or item can hold traces of its energy and can be used thereafter in magic to influence it. Something like a footprint or a piece of clothing falls into this category; likewise, the age-old idea of using someone's hair or nail clippings is an example of contagious magic. When separated, things once united or paired can be used as a connection between them. If you've seen BFF necklaces—a pendant is snapped in two, and each friend wears half—that's another form of contagious magic. The two people become connected by the halves of the pendant, just as they are connected by friendship.

WORD MAGIC AND AFFIRMATIONS

Word magic is a very direct way to do spellwork. The easiest way to use word magic is to speak aloud, phrasing your magic in an active way, stating your desired reality as already achieved. For example, instead of saying, "I will be brave," say, "I am brave."

Affirmations can be a powerful form of word magic. Repeating something is a method of constructing a new reality. They're particularly useful in altering an attitude toward something.

Affirmations are ideal for working to protect prosperity and financial situations; for self-esteem and confidence issues; for expanding awareness; and for enhancing your intuition, all of which contribute to better self-defense.

Like other word magic, an affirmation should always be phrased in the present tense and spoken in positive terms. "I am safe" signifies to your subconscious mind that you are protected right now and you have only to realize it, whereas "I will be safe" sends the message that your protection will always lie sometime in the future, never now. "I'm not scared" doesn't work as well as "I am courageous," mainly because your mind grabs onto the key concept of fear rather than the negative that accompanies it.

Another aspect of word magic is the written form. Written magic is easy to do. Take a piece of new paper of whatever size you like and write out your desire or statement. You can fold it and put it under a candle, burn it, roll it up and tie a thread around it and carry it as a talisman, or fold it up and tuck it into a locket. Use colored paper to add another level of energy or use colored inks or patterned paper from a craft store in a motif that supports your spell's goal. The possibilities are endless.

Writing something out over and over is another physical reinforcement of the energy of a thought, like speaking something aloud. Both use physical action to underscore a concept that exists in your mind. Written magic can be carving words on a candle, writing key words on a slip of paper to carry as a talisman or amulet, or creating a piece of magical art to display in your home. (The Himmelsbrief in Chapter 3 is a terrific example of this.)

AFFIRM THE POSITIVE

Affirmations are positive statements, but the point about creating a new reality is also valid for negative statements. If you constantly make negative remarks about yourself or believe the negative things others say about you, that works to create a reality that you really don't want. The very word *affirmation* reflects the positive nature of this technique. You affirm, or support, the new reality that you desire to manifest.

KEEPING RECORDS

It's all well and good to toss spells around. But what makes you an effective and successful spellcaster is paying attention to what works and what doesn't work. If something doesn't work, examine the potential reasons it might have failed. Keep notes regarding what day of the week or time of day you cast the spell. (Maybe lunchtime spellwork always fizzles.) What components/supplies did you use? (Perhaps rosemary is a no-go herb for you because its energy and yours don't get along.) There is no point in wasting time and energy on a spell that isn't going to work, and the only way to figure out how to save time is by keeping track of your successes and failures.

Grab a notebook and start noting the date and time, the weather, the ingredients/supplies/elements you used, the phase of the moon, your mood, your health—anything and everything you can think of. Write down how you felt while casting the spell and how you felt after you were done, and make sure to note any effects that manifest later, such as odd dreams, unexpected fatigue, or amped-up energy levels. Leave space to note results, if any, when you notice them. All this information provides you with a body of knowledge to review for insight into the strengths and weaknesses in your spellcasting.

PART 2:
SPELLS

CHAPTER 2:
BODY AND SPIRIT

Responsibility for protection starts with yourself. In today's society, people are under a constant barrage of negative energy, besieged physically, mentally, and emotionally by environmental drains, social stress, and having to keep up with life's demands. The first step toward dealing with it all is to protect yourself from the onslaught.

It's no secret that mental and emotional exhaustion can affect you physically. These three areas are irrevocably intertwined. As a result, a lot of the areas these spells are designed to focus on can overlap. For example, if you have a high-maintenance associate, he or she may draw on you mentally and emotionally, which can negatively impact your physical energy. Until you are more experienced in spellcasting, address these issues separately at first to help you really focus on the defined goal. Later, you can fold them all into a single spell.

MAGIC HELPS THOSE WHO HELP THEMSELVES

Magic isn't the sole answer to a problem. You can't use spellcraft to protect your home and then go out leaving all your windows open and the door unlocked. You need to work to support it outside the spell as well. That means keeping certain things about protecting yourself in mind:

- **Use common sense.** Stay away from dangerous areas. Know where you're going at all times and familiarize yourself with the layout or directions ahead of time. Let someone know where you're going and what time you expect to be back and make sure you have contact numbers for people in case of an emergency.

- **If you know certain people tire you out physically or energy-wise, limit the time you spend with them.** These people have an energy imbalance and absorb energy from wherever they can, and they often don't know they're doing it. Sometimes you can have the opposite problem and feel overwhelmed by an outgoing person who forcefully projects energy. He or she may not be doing it aggressively; he or she might just be exuberant or really like you! However, these people can be tiring too.

- **Remain calm in a situation that scares you.** If you start to panic, you will get tangled up in your own fear and make protecting yourself harder.

- **Remember that a deliberate psychic attack is very, very rare.** Self-jinxing is actually the most common affliction, far more common than someone else dedicated to investing all that energy into ruining your life. Don't fool yourself into thinking you're under psychic attack or being dogged by bad luck. It's a self-fulfilling prophecy, and you'll start attracting negativity, perpetuating the cycle. Break it with magic instead.

GENERAL SELF-PROTECTION

This section begins with the most basic of protection techniques. If a vicious dog is racing at you, the safest thing to do is to slam a door shut between you, with you inside and the dog outside. The magical equivalent of this is raising a shield around yourself, a protective sphere or container of energy to keep danger on the outside and you on the inside. Where does this energy come from? Inside you and around you.

The first few spells in this book are the equivalent of learning how to boil water before venturing into making pasta or hard-boiled eggs. They're basic techniques that should be the first things you do before leaving your house or even leaving your bed if you live in a place where you feel unsafe somehow.

CENTERING AND GROUNDING

Centering refers to finding your core and calmly focusing on your own energy within yourself; it's a form of mindfulness. *Grounding* refers to connecting that core to the earth's energy, enabling you to balance out your energy levels. Centering and grounding are both very common practices also found in meditation and martial arts.

Centering and Grounding

A sure way to exhaust yourself is to use all your own energy to do magic. By connecting to a larger energy source, you can allow that energy to flow through you, nourishing your own energy levels as well as powering what you're doing magically. This technique is also essential any time you feel frightened or panicked. It secures you and reinforces your stability, allowing you to face whatever's happening with balance and equanimity.

What to Do:

1. Sit or stand comfortably and close your eyes. Take three deep breaths.
2. Visualize a glowing light in the core of your body. You can locate it wherever feels right; most people instinctively visualize it at the heart or abdominal level.
3. Visualize this glowing light extending a tendril down toward the earth, passing through the ground and deep into the earth's core. See it meet and join with the energy of the earth.
4. Visualize the energy of the earth traveling up the tendril to re-energize your own core. Feel the energy suffusing you, nourishing your energy levels, redressing any energy imbalances you are suffering, and stabilizing you. You are connected to the earth.
5. Maintain this connection for as long as you wish, enjoying the communication of energy. When it is time, thank the earth for sharing its energy and reduce the flow of energy but don't completely close off the energy conduit between the earth and your core. Allow it to remain a thread connecting you so you can draw up energy at will or shunt off excess energy if you need to.

TIP

- If it helps, imagine your own energy as one color and the earth's energy as another. When you draw the earth's energy up to ground yourself, imagine the color of that earth energy mingling with the color of your own energy.

You can also perform this in reverse if you feel as if you have too much energy. Follow the visualization through to the connection with the energy at the earth's core. Instead of drawing earth energy up, however, visualize the excess energy in you flowing *down*.

Basic Shield

Once you know how to center and ground, you can use the earth's energy to form a shield around yourself. This is very similar to the Basic Circle Cast in Chapter 1. You can extend the shield as far as you like; just be aware that the bigger you make it, the harder it may be to maintain. For a personal shield, start with a bubble that you could touch with the tips of your fingers if you held your arms out to your sides.

What to Do:

1. Center and ground. Draw the earth's energy up into your core.
2. Visualize the energy in your core expanding outward past your physical body like a soap bubble. Expand it to the desired diameter.
3. To help secure your visualization, you can speak a key phrase, such as, *"I invoke my personal shield. No danger or ill befalls me, safe within its protection."*

TIPS

- You'll find that a personal energy shield will naturally degrade as the day goes on. Check it often, extending your awareness to sense if there are any weak spots. If there are, simply draw up more earth energy and reinforce the entire shield.

- It may seem like a good idea to make a permanent shield, but it isn't. A shield can rust in place, making it difficult for you to pass energy you *want* to access in and out of it. Lower your shield regularly and make a new one so you can lower it at a moment's notice if you need to.

Advanced Personal Shield

Once you have mastered erecting a basic personal shield, you can experiment with various tweaks to find a shield that really resonates with you and your needs. Try this mirrored variation.

What to Do:

Once you have shaped your personal shield, imagine the soap bubble–like surface turning into a mirror, reflective side out. This will bounce negativity away from you.

Experiment with other surfaces to your shield. Why not try a net of vines woven around your shield? What happens if you visualize it as a sphere of ice? Sunlight? Flowing water? Find what works best for you. (And that may change from day to day or according to what kind of environment you find yourself in.)

Waxing Moon Spell

Traditionally, the first half of the moon cycle, when the moon waxes from dark to full, is associated with drawing things toward you. This is an ideal time to work on inviting positive energy into your life: healthy body, healthy mind, happy heart, strong financial situation, focus, resilience…whatever you think you need. This version focuses on general protection.

What You Need:
Small white candle, such as a tea light or birthday candle
Candleholder (a lump of putty works for the birthday candle)
Matches or lighter

What to Do:

1. Center and ground.
2. Place the candle in the holder and light it. Say, *"Waxing moon, bring me protection from all that seeks to harm me. Thank you for your many blessings."*
3. Allow the candle to burn down.

TIP

- You can use this as a basis for a specific spell targeting protection from a specific issue. Just identify it in place of saying, *"from all that seeks to harm me."*

Waning Moon Spell

The second half of the moon phase is when the moon wanes from full to dark. This is the time traditionally associated with banishing, reversing, or getting rid of things. It's easy to tweak the previous spell to be performed in the waning phase just by rephrasing your wish.

What You Need:

Small white candle, such as a tea light or birthday candle
Candleholder (a lump of putty works for the birthday candle)
Matches or lighter

What to Do:

1. Center and ground.
2. Place the candle in the holder and light it. Say, *"Waning moon, banish from my life all that seeks to harm me. Thank you for your many blessings."*
3. Allow the candle to burn down.

TIP

- White candles are multipurpose. If you prefer to use a black candle and can find a small one, go ahead and use that for the banishing version. Or use any other color that you associate with banishing.

PROTECTING YOURSELF PHYSICALLY

While most of the spells in this chapter are designed around protecting you, these spells focus specifically on protecting your physical body, be it from physical harm or a physical effect of negative energy.

Poppet Spell

A poppet is a small doll or figure of a human used as a focus for magic. In this spell, it's meant to represent your physical body, and serves as the focus for your energy. In the past, poppets were carved from wood, sewn from scraps of material, and even made of roots or rope twisted together. This spell uses felt. You can use a color of your choice; choose either your favorite or a color associated with protection, such as red, black, or blue. If you have a gingerbread man (or woman!) cookie cutter, you can use that as a template for the shape.

Otherwise, freehand a simple human shape. The second part of the spell creates a box to store the poppet in.

What You Need:

2 squares of felt, approximately 6 inches × 6 inches

Sharpie marker

Straight pins

Scissors

Needle and thread

Yarn, scraps of clothing (optional)

6–12 cotton balls

Penny or other coin from your birth year

Pinch of salt

Pinch of rosemary

Pinch of rue

Red jasper

What to Do:

1. Stack the two pieces of felt one on top of the other and draw the outline of a human shape with the Sharpie. Pin the pieces of felt together, then cut out the shape.
2. Stitch the two pieces together around the edges, leaving the head open.
3. Use the Sharpie to draw features and physical characteristics on the shape. If you have a scar or a birthmark or always wear a specific piece of jewelry, draw it. The idea is to make the poppet look like you by using key identifying elements. Add yarn for hair if you like or stitch on clothes from scraps of your own old clothing.
4. Tease out the cotton balls a bit, then start slipping them into the poppet. When you are halfway done, add the penny, pinches of salt, rosemary, and rue, then the red jasper. Finish stuffing the

poppet with the remaining cotton balls. Pin the head shut and stitch it closed.

5. Center and ground. Hold the poppet in your hands and draw energy up to the ground, filling your core. Let your energy trickle down your arms to the poppet in your hands. Say, *"This poppet is me; as it is kept safe, so am I kept safe."*

TIPS

- If you're drawing your poppet freehand, don't get too detailed or make the arms and legs too long or narrow; they'll be hard to stuff. Keep it a generic outline. Think gingerbread man, and you'll be on the right track.

- If you like, you can add a strand or two of your hair or a couple of nail clippings into the poppet as you insert the other ingredients.

Poppet Box

This spell creates a safe place for your poppet to be stored.

What You Need:
Wooden box with lid, large enough to hold the poppet
Black paint
Paintbrush
White cloth, large enough to wrap the poppet

What to Do:

1. Paint the inside of the box with the black paint. Don't forget the inside of the lid. Allow to dry.
2. Wrap the poppet in the white cloth and set it inside the box. Close the lid. Repeat, *"As this poppet is safe, so am I kept safe."*
3. Put the box in a safe place.

The poppet box project can also make an excellent general spell box. Many of the spells in this book call for something to be kept in a safe place. A spell box is a great idea to house these objects. Make a general spell box to keep them safe.

TIP

- You can stain or paint the outside of the poppet box as well if you choose or decorate it however you like. Consider gluing a mirror to the top of the box, programmed to reflect negative energy away from the poppet (and therefore you).

Protection Amulet

The wearing of protective symbols keyed to your beliefs is an age-old practice. Choose a piece of jewelry that you already wear or get a new one that you can dedicate to this specific purpose. Either way, cleanse the jewelry by passing it through incense smoke before performing the spell in order to remove foreign energy and any energy buildup before programming it with this new purpose.

What You Need:

Stick or cone of incense (sandalwood or frankincense) and censer or incense boat

Matches or lighter

Item of jewelry

What to Do:

1. Center and ground.
2. Light the incense. Pass the item of jewelry through the smoke, saying, *"By the power of this purifying incense, you are cleansed of all prior negative energy."*

3. Hold the item in your hands. Close your eyes and draw energy up from the earth, feeling it flow down your arms. Direct the energy into the item, saying, *"I charge you, [item], to be for me a shield, a defense against injury and danger."*

4. Wear the item as often as possible—certainly every time you go out.

TIP

- Before you put the item of jewelry on, take a purifying bath or shower or do another of the energy-cleansing spells in this chapter to start with a clean slate.

If you don't have a symbol that you associate with protection or don't feel comfortable wearing it publicly, choose a plain piece of jewelry that you will be able to wear. Don't stress too much about your choice; you can deconsecrate the amulet and make a new one as your taste evolves. On the other hand, an amulet can collect more power as it is worn and used, and the point of using jewelry is that it isn't disposable.

Lemon Cleanse

You wash your face every night and your hands regularly…why not do a regular wipe down of any negative energy that has accumulated too? You can do this in the shower or anytime as a quick reset. Lemon is a traditional antidote to negative energy.

What You Need:
Lemon slice

What to Do:

1. Envision any negative energy clinging to your body or aura collecting at the back of your neck. Visualize it as black or a murky brown, if that helps. (This may feel uncomfortable. Don't worry. You're about to get rid of it.)
2. Wipe the slice of lemon over the back of your neck, allowing it to absorb all the negative energy. Wipe for as long as you feel necessary.
3. Toss the lemon slice in the compost where it will decompose, and the energy it removed from you will be transformed.

TIP

• If the feeling of negative energy at the back of your neck is too disturbing, call it to collect in the palm of one of your hands, then use the lemon to wipe it off.

Purifying Bath

Sometimes you need more than a quick fix. A purifying bath can help you relax. The blend of salt, rosemary, and sandalwood will help remove any negative energy clinging to you and reset your energy.

What You Need:

1 cup Epsom salt
1 teaspoon rosemary

3 drops sandalwood
essential oil

What to Do:

1. Mix all the ingredients in a small bowl.
2. Draw a bath at a comfortable temperature. Sprinkle the Epsom salt blend under the running water.
3. Soak in the bath for as long as you like.

Smudging

Smudging is a traditional method of purification used in several cultures. A bundle of dried herbs is lit and the flame extinguished, leaving the herbal matter to smoke. Sage is one of the traditional purifying herbs and the most common kind of smudge stick you'll find.

What You Need:
Smudge stick
Matches or lighter
Heatproof bowl

What to Do:

1. Light the end of the smudge stick. Gently blow out the flame once the dried herbal matter has caught. You may hold the smudge stick in your hand for this, lay it in the heatproof dish and hold the dish itself, or place the dish on a table next to you. Whatever is easiest!

2. Gently waft the smoke up and down your body. Cup your hand and use a washing motion, spreading the smoke along your arms and legs. As you do, visualize the smoke dissolving any unwanted energy clinging to you.

You don't have to use an entire smudge stick. When you've finished purifying the space or energy, extinguish the stick by tamping it out in a heatproof bowl or sand. When it's cool, wrap it in foil and keep it till the next time you need it.

Sunlight Spell

Never underestimate the power of sunlight! This is a quick, easy, and direct spell to use when you're in a difficult situation. It's easiest to perform on a sunny day, but even on an overcast day, the sun is up there, just behind the clouds.

What to Do:

1. If you feel anxious, threatened, or unsafe in some way, make your way outside to stand in the fresh air.
2. Lift your face to the sun and close your eyes. Say, *"Sun, banish this negative energy. Break its hold upon me."*
3. Feel the warmth of the sun on your face and body. Breathe slowly and deeply, imagining the sunlight flowing into your body with every inhalation.
4. Say, *"I am free. Thank you, sun."*
5. Return to your situation and carry on with your day. If you ended your involvement and excused yourself, you can move on to another location.

TIP

- It's best to do this outside, but in a pinch, you can walk to a window and stand facing it, pulling in the energy of the sunlight through the glass.

Do you have to speak the words of a spell aloud? It helps, because talking is a physical act that can help underscore your intent, but if you're in a situation in which you have to remain silent, then go ahead and speak the words inside your mind. Or you can subvocalize them, moving your lips and your vocal cords without actually producing sound.

Large Witches' Ladder

A witches' ladder is a spell technique that involves knot magic. This ladder focuses on protecting the place in which it is hung or the person for whom it is made. This version makes a larger braid that can be hung on a wall or tucked in a drawer.

What You Need:

3 (3-foot) lengths of cord, yarn, string, wool, or embroidery thread
Beads, feathers, small pendant charms associated with protection
Needle and thread (optional; see instructions)

What to Do:

1. Tie the three lengths of cord together at one end.
2. Visualizing your goal, slowly begin to braid the three cords together.
3. Whenever you feel it is right, pause in the braiding to slip a bead over one of the cords or slide a small charm over one of the threads. If your cords are too thick to slide through the beads and charms, finish braiding the entire lengths of cord and tie them off. Then, using the needle and thread, sew the beads and charms to the braid at various intervals. Weave the feathers into the braid or sew them on.
4. Hang the witches' ladder in the area you wish protected. You may loop it and tie the ends together to make a circle and hang it like a wreath or hang it vertically by one of the knots. Alternatively, you can fold or coil it up and slip it into a small space.

TIPS

• Check Chapter 7 to look up colors and symbols associated with protection in various settings to help you choose things to weave into the braid. Symbols of shields, weapons, or animals you associate with defense are all good ideas too.

- It may help to hold the tied end of the cords down with something heavy before you start braiding or to tape them to a table. You could also pin the knot to a pillow or sofa cushion.

Knot magic uses the act of tying or twisting cord together to secure magic and energy in the knots.

Mini Witches' Ladder

This is a small personal-sized witches' ladder that you can carry in a pocket or purse. It's best to use lighter cord, yarn, or string for this version. As in the previous spell, if your cord is too thick for the beads or charms, sew them on in the places indicated instead.

What You Need:
3 (1-foot) lengths of cord, yarn, string, wool, or embroidery thread
3 beads or small pendant charms associated with protection

What to Do:
1. Tie the three lengths of cord together at one end.
2. Slip a bead or charm on the center cord right underneath the knot.
3. Visualizing your goal, slowly begin to braid the three cords together.
4. Just before the halfway point, slip another charm or bead onto a cord. Continue braiding.
5. About an inch before the end, slip the final bead or charm onto a cord. Knot the ends together.

6. Carry the witches' ladder with you. You may loop it and tie the ends together to make a circle, coil it up, or just tuck it into a small space.

TIP

• These mini ladders make great protective charms for luggage when you travel. Tuck one inside your suitcase the next time you take a trip!

Trap Negativity

If you're out and about and you start feeling unnerved or uncomfortable or you start a spiral of negative thinking, try this quick spell. You can use the end of a shoelace, the loose end of a strap on a backpack, or anything at all. In a pinch you can even use a shirttail, a scarf, or a purse strap.

What You Need:
1 cord, any length

What to Do:

1. When you feel anger or fear rising inside or sense something not quite right around you, visualize that negative energy fusing into a ball in front of you. Hold the length of cord taut between your fingers and say, *"I command you to halt; I bind you where you are. You cannot harm me."*
2. Tie the cord into a simple slipknot, visualizing the cord being tied around the ball of negative energy in front of you. Holding the cord taut, inhale deeply, then exhale and let the tension leave your body. Release the cord to dangle freely again.
3. When you have moved on to a safe place, untie the knot and allow the energy to disperse.

PROTECTING YOUR HEALTH

Health is a key area to support with magic. This is a different issue than the basic protection or physical protection covered earlier, in that this section focuses on maintaining health or specifically addressing health issues. Health is part of the overall puzzle that contributes to well-being. By protecting your health, you're helping protect everything else in your life as well.

Medical Bureaucracy

Part of maintaining health is dealing with the medical establishment, and sometimes there is red tape. Nothing is more distressing than having to struggle with bureaucracy when you are already worried about illness, well-being, and financial security, either your own or that of a family member. Here's a spell to help untangle that red tape and smooth out the paperwork.

What You Need:
Blank paper, approximately 4 inches × 4 inches
Pen or pencil
Red yarn, 8–10 inches long
Scissors

What to Do:

1. Center and ground.
2. On the paper, write the medical procedure that you need performed or the bill you need to claim on your insurance. Fold up the paper and tie the red yarn around it as many times as you can.
3. Say, *"From out of the maze of red tape, from the black hole of bureaucracy, into the light of success: obstacles are no more!"*

4. Cut the red yarn into pieces small enough that you can't tie them in knots anymore. Unfold the paper and say, *"Communication flows, success is mine."*
5. Dispose of the shredded yarn in the trash. Keep the paper until the procedure is scheduled or the insurance payment is secured, then burn it and scatter the ashes outside.

TIP

• You may have to do this spell more than once, as new obstacles may arise in the process. Use new red yarn each time but refold the original paper until the entire situation is definitely past.

Citrus and Clove Spell for Better Health

This may be a familiar craft from your childhood, often practiced around the Christmas season. Here it invokes the associations citrus has with health and the association cloves have with anesthetic and purification.

What You Need:
Small orange or lemon
Jar of whole cloves
Plate
Thin skewer or pushpin (optional; see instructions)
Small dish

What to Do:

1. Center and ground.
2. Hold the fruit in your hands and say, *"[Fruit], I call upon your healing and strengthening energy."*
3. Working over the plate to catch any juice that runs, begin pushing whole cloves into the peel of the fruit, one by one. If the peel is

too hard or the cloves too dull, use the skewer or pushpin to make small guide holes first.

4. Cover as much of the surface of the fruit as you can with the cloves. When you are done, hold the fruit in your hands and say, *"Protect my health, citrus and cloves."*

5. Place the fruit in the small dish and put it in a place with good airflow. Turn it every day to allow it to dry evenly. If it starts to mold instead, compost it and create another one. (Don't worry; this has nothing to do with the state of your health and everything to do with how damp or dry your climate is.)

6. Once it has dried, keep the clove-studded orange in the dish for as long as you feel it is required. Do check it regularly to make sure it's still all right; if it discolors, molds, or otherwise goes bad, compost it and create a new one. If you keep it in a place of high-energy traffic, you might consider making a new one every three to four months.

TIPS

- You can create designs on the orange with the cloves instead of covering it completely, if you wish. Bear in mind that the fewer cloves there are, the shorter the lifespan of the orange.

- You can hang the orange up after it has dried; make a loop with a piece of ribbon and use a couple of sewing pins to attach it to the orange.

Salt Spell to Draw Out Illness or Infection

Salt draws away negative energy. This spell can be performed when you are ill to help draw the illness out of your body.

What You Need:
Salt
Small bowl

What to Do:

1. Center and ground.
2. Place the salt in the bowl and place the bowl on the region or part of the body that is afflicted by the illness or damage. Allow it to stay there for at least 3 minutes, preferably longer, to absorb the negative energy that is collected there. Visualize the infection or damage as dark, murky energy rising up through your body and being drawn into the salt.
3. Alternatively, if you have a virus or general infection, hold the bowl in front of your mouth and exhale completely into it. Do this three times, visualizing the illness in your body as a murky cloud leaving your body via your breath and being directed into the salt.
4. Dispose of the salt by flushing it down the toilet.

TIP

- If a bowl is awkward, pour salt into a small disposable/compostable tea bag and use that instead.

Salt Spell to Cleanse a Sickroom

Are you bedbound because you're sick? This is an easy spell to help cleanse the unhealthy energy from your sickroom.

What You Need:
Salt
Small bowl

What to Do:

1. Place the salt in the bowl. Say, *"Salt, I call upon you to absorb illness and negative energy from this room."*
2. Place the bowl of salt under your bed. Replace it daily, disposing of the used salt by flushing it down the toilet.

Sun Spell for Health and Healing

Bask in the sun! Sometimes you lack the energy to do something more active. This spell is a terrific way to use the sun's energy to support your healing or to maintain good health. This can be performed inside sitting by a sunny window or outside if the temperature is agreeable.

What You Need:
Sunny day

What to Do:

1. Position yourself in the sun. If possible, orient the part of your body that needs the healing energy toward the warmth of the sun; otherwise, just sit in the sunlight.
2. Say aloud (or in your head): *"Sun, I call upon your healing energy to aid me."* If you have a specific ailment you wish the sun to help with, name it here.
3. With your eyes closed, breathe deeply and evenly. Feel the warmth of the sun on your skin. Visualize the sunlight melting into your body. Imagine it seeping into your cells, traveling from one to the next, glowing with health. Sit there as long as you wish or feel you need to.

TIP

* If you fall asleep during this spell, don't worry. Sleep brings healing too.

Protecting Yourself from Physical Exhaustion

Physical exhaustion is a common problem in contemporary society. People push and push and push, trying to meet the needs of family, job, running the house, and lastly, their own self-care. Often, you don't have time—or, sadly, the energy available—to recharge. This spell can help manage your energy levels and keep you from physical exhaustion.

What You Need:

1 teaspoon light oil (such as almond or sunflower)
Pinch of dried lavender
Pinch of ground cinnamon

Brown jasper
Clear quartz crystal
Black pouch or bag

What to Do:

1. Center and ground.
2. Add the dried herbs to the oil and swirl to combine.
3. Hold the stones in your hands and say, *"Stamina, endurance, fortitude: I am protected from depletion and exhaustion. I always have enough energy. Brown jasper defends my stamina; clear quartz ensures I always have energy to draw on. It is so!"*
4. Dip your finger in the herbed oil and anoint each stone. Slip them into the black bag and close it.
5. Carry the bag with you.

TIPS

- To renew the spell, repeat it monthly with the same words. You can repeat the anointing or not as you choose.

- Add a pinch of dried lavender and ground cinnamon to the bag with the stones if you like.

Defending Your Energy from Being Drained

When your energy is being siphoned off, the first signs are usually physical. Fatigue, slowing down, and a general dull feeling can all suggest a loss of essential energy, either to others leeching it or by the energy leaking in general. This spell can help you guard your energy from interference and loss.

What You Need:
Quartz crystal

What to Do:

1. Cleanse the stone according to your preferred method from Chapter 7.
2. Center and ground.
3. Hold the stone. Draw energy up from the ground and let it flow down your arms to the stone in your hands. Say, *"Quartz, with your endless power and energy, support my energy; defend it from being stolen or lost."*
4. Carry the stone with you.

TIP

- Quartz jewelry is easy to find. A quartz pendant could be slipped onto your keychain or used as a zipper pull on your purse or backpack—whatever you carry with you.

Charm Bag Against Fatigue

Mugwort is a traditional herb to use against fatigue. This quick and easy charm bag calls on its energy to help fight weariness and lethargy.

What You Need:
Mugwort   Small black pouch

What to Do:

1. Ground and center.
2. Hold your hand over the mugwort and say, *"Creature of earth, I charge you to defend me from exhaustion, to ensure my energy is always high, to guard against fatigue."*

3. Put the mugwort into the black pouch and tie it shut.
4. Carry the pouch of mugwort with you.

For an extra zing, combine the mugwort spell with the quartz spell and create a charm bag to defend your energy and ward off exhaustion. This is a terrific combo for draining work environments.

Safe Medical Procedure

Sometimes, as much as you may trust a doctor, it's reassuring to work some magic to safeguard a medical procedure, such as surgery or childbirth. This spell uses runes drawn on your body with salt water. (For more information about runes, see Chapter 7.)

What You Need:
Small dish   1 teaspoon salt
¼ cup water

What to Do:

1. Pour the water into the dish. Stir the salt into the water with your finger. Draw a spiral in it starting from the outside of the dish and spiraling clockwise to the inside, then lift your finger straight out. Repeat this twice more, for a total of three times.
2. On each spiral, say one of these statements:

   My surgeon/doctor is secure.
   My procedure is successful.
   My recovery is assured.

3. With a wet finger, draw Ansuz, the rune of success, on your forehead, over your heart, and on your abdomen, dipping your finger into the water again each time.

4. Dip your finger one more time into the salt water, then draw Thurisaz, the rune of protection and overcoming obstacles, on the part of your body that will be the focus of the procedure. Say, *"My body is blessed; white light shines about me. I am protected; my safety is defended."*

TIP

- A good companion spell to this one is the creation of an amulet for health (see earlier in this chapter). Bring the amulet into the hospital with you. You won't be able to wear or carry it into your procedure, but you can place it under or next to a photograph of you in your hospital room.

Protection from Miscarriage

Knot magic is particularly efficient at binding something, and it's an excellent technique to use to help support a pregnancy. You can perform this spell yourself if you are pregnant or for someone else. If you can't be with them, have a photo of them on hand.

Important! If you perform this spell, you must remember to perform the last part to unknot the cord and remove any obstacle to the birth. Don't just tuck the cord away and forget about it, or it may present complications during labor!

What You Need:
White cord, approximately 6–10 inches long
Small red pouch

What to Do:

1. Ground and center.
2. Hold the cord to your belly or against the photo of the mother-to-be. Then tie a knot in the cord, visualizing the knot tying the pregnancy in place, keeping the baby safe and healthy.
3. Say, *"Be safe; hold fast. Let the womb guard you till the time has come to be brought safely into this world."*
4. Tuck the cord into the red pouch and keep it safe. If there are complications during the pregnancy, you can use this as a focus for further protective magic.
5. A couple of weeks before the due date (or whenever the decision is made to bring the child to birth), fetch the pouch. Ground and center, then remove the cord from the pouch. Untie the knot, saying, *"Your time draws near; be free to come safely to our loving arms, in full health."*

TIP

- For extra protection, slip a cowrie shell or two into the red pouch along with the cord. Cowrie shells are associated with women in general and fertility and pregnancy specifically.

Sometimes a pregnancy goes wrong despite all possible support. If the pregnancy terminates, undo the knot so the mother doesn't suffer anymore emotional pain or physical trauma than she has to. Thank the child's spirit and bury the cord with reverence.

Banishing Illness

If you feel yourself coming down with something or have an illness that has been dragging on, this is a good spell to use to kick it to the curb.

What to Do:

1. Stand if you can; otherwise, sit up in bed.
2. Center and ground.
3. Through your connection with the energy of the earth, draw up energy from the ground and collect it in your hands.
4. Start stroking your hands over your body, about an inch or two away from the skin, visualizing illness being washed away by the energy. As you do, say, *"Away, [illness], this is not your abode. Away to the depths of the sea, away to the highest of mountains; away."*
5. When you are done, kneel down and place your hands on the floor. Allow the energy to drain away. Draw up new energy from the ground to redress any imbalance that may have come about during your spell.
6. Wash your hands or just hold them under running water at the sink to help clear away the last parts of the energy work you did.

Running water is a great way to shake negativity in a pinch. Place your hands under a stream of water from a faucet and visualize any negativity flowing away.

PROTECTING YOUR MENTAL HEALTH

Humans are fragile creatures, and our thought processes can be worn down by fear, stress, and low self-confidence. Spellwork can help reinforce your clarity of thought, your self-esteem, and your ability to trust yourself in the minefield of today's negative environments.

Affirmations

Affirmations are positive statements used to reinforce a reality or to strengthen an area of weakness. Here is a list of affirmations you can use to protect your self-esteem, or you can write your own.

- I am strong and worthy of respect.
- I am centered and balanced. I am in harmony with my surroundings.
- I deserve to be heard.

What to Do:

1. Stand or sit squarely. Relax, but don't flop. Your affirmation is going to address strength; hold yourself confidently, but don't hold onto tension.
2. Center and ground.
3. Close your eyes and take three slow, deep breaths, exhaling steadily after each.
4. Speak your chosen affirmation, preferably aloud. If you are in a group of people, subvocalize or think the affirmation firmly. Speak confidently. Say the affirmation at least three times.
5. Feel yourself surrounded by a feeling of confidence and strength that increases with each repetition of your affirmation.
6. Open your eyes and return to your situation.

Clarity of Thought

If you find yourself muddled and unable to think through a problem, this spell will help encourage clear thinking. It can help cut through the fog and protect your ability to think clearly.

What You Need:

Yellow candle and candleholder

Lemon oil

Matches or lighter

Citrine

What to Do:

1. Center and ground.
2. Hold the candle in your hands and say, *"Yellow candle, be the light that clears the fog."* Dab it with the lemon oil and say, *"Lemon bright, cut through the darkness."* Place the candle in the holder and light it.
3. Take the citrine and hold it between your hands. Visualize yourself confidently handling a problem, working through a challenging project, being complimented on your productivity. Rub a drop of lemon oil over the citrine, saying, *"Yellow stone, lemon bright, be my insight."*
4. Place the citrine at the base of the candle and allow the candle to burn down.
5. Carry the stone with you to benefit from its energy.

Saying No

Saying no to something or someone can be incredibly difficult. Sometimes you genuinely want to help, but you have to refuse because of other commitments. Other times you want to refuse but feel guilty and as if you have to say yes. Either way, not saying no means you end up with too much on your plate or handling something you don't want to be involved with. This spell can strengthen your resolve and help you say no with kindness and confidence. You don't owe anyone an explanation beyond, "I'm sorry, I just can't take that on right now."

What You Need:
Silver candle with holder
Matches or lighter
Rose quartz
Jasper (color your choice; green or red recommended)
Black tourmaline
1 teaspoon honey

What to Do:

1. Center and ground.
2. Light the candle, saying, *"My time has value. My life balance has value. My energy has value."*
3. Set the stones in a triangle around the candle. Place the rose quartz in front and the other two stones to either side behind the candle.
4. Dip your finger into the honey and touch the rose quartz, saying, *"I deserve to live guilt-free about my choices. I am my own person with the right to make my own decisions."*
5. Dip your finger in the honey again and touch the jasper, saying, *"I balance my activities to the best of my ability. Each area of my life deserves its own space and attention. I will not rob time or energy from any of them to satisfy someone else's expectations."*
6. Dip your finger in the honey a third time and touch the black tourmaline, saying, *"My energy is my own. It belongs to no one but the people I choose to give it to. It is protected from those who would steal it or abuse it."*
7. Allow the candle to burn down.

TIP

- You can carry these stones in a pouch to have their energy with you to help support your resolution. You may want to wrap them in a small scrap of white or blue cloth first so the sticky honey doesn't gum up the inside of the pouch.

Green jasper is a good stone to use when working for balance between different areas of your life. Red jasper also helps with balance and with strengthening boundaries. Use one or both in this spell.

Trusting Yourself

Gaslighting, negging (insults disguised as backhanded compliments intended to attack your self-confidence), and other constant external attacks on your self-worth can make trusting yourself a challenge. If you're in a situation where someone is manipulating you like this, deliberately or otherwise, use this spell to strengthen your sense of self and remind yourself that you're worthy of positive recognition. You can use any size plate; just adjust the number of tea lights.

What You Need:

Plate

Tea light candles (enough to form a circle around the inside edge of the plate)

Matches or lighter

Rose quartz

Tiger's eye

Obsidian

Black pouch

What to Do:

1. Set the tea light candles up on the plate, forming a circle around the inside edge. Place the three stones in the middle.
2. Light the candles.
3. Say, *"I am a calm, rational person with valid concerns. I know my truth, and I speak it."*
4. Leave the stones in the circle of candles until the candles have burned out. Then slip them into the black pouch and carry it with you.

Tiger's eye is a stone that reinforces courage and strength. It's ideal to use in a spell like this.

PROTECTING YOURSELF FROM MENTAL EXHAUSTION

Mental burnout is no fun. And often you can't see that it's happening until you're well on your way to being wrecked. Overstudying, having to take in too much information in a short span of time, and burnout are all situations that you can use spellwork to cope with. Try some of these spells to protect yourself from overdoing it.

Defending Against Decision Paralysis

Decision paralysis is the inability to make a decision due to anxiety, fatigue, or overthinking the situation. Being afraid that you will make the incorrect choice can trap you into freezing up, making you unable to move forward. This spell helps you own your personal power to make your choices—*any* choices.

What You Need:

White candle

Bamboo skewer, long nail,
 or ice pick

Candleholder

Matches or lighter

What to Do:

1. Center and ground.
2. Take the candle in your hand. With the skewer, nail, or ice pick, starting at the bottom of the candle, scratch or carve the phrase "My choices are mine to make" into the candle.
3. Set the candle in the candleholder and light it. Say, *"I am grounded. My choices are mine. One choice does not negate all the others. Perfection is not the goal. What matters is that I step forward."*
4. Watch the candle for a time, breathing deeply and feeling your energy pulsing in your core. Imagine yourself making a choice with confidence and things unfolding in a positive fashion. Day-dream about being confident in your decisions. When you are ready, repeat, *"Perfection is not the goal. What matters is that I step forward."*
5. Allow the candle to burn out.

TIP

- If it helps, write out the affirmation from Step 3 on a small paper or blank business card and carry it with you. Read it often. If you find yourself paralyzed by decisions, close your eyes, repeat the words to yourself either aloud or in your head, and remember that the choice doesn't have to be perfect; it just has to be made so you can move forward.

Protection from Oversaturation

When studying or otherwise taking in a lot of information, you can easily get overwhelmed. Use this spell to help strengthen your ability to survive the onslaught of information and even retain the important parts. Studying too much or researching too much can lead to information overload. This spell can help you reinforce your ability to process and retain the material you need to. Brown jasper is associated with strength and long-term endurance, which is just the kind of energy you want helping you in situations like this.

What You Need:
Brown jasper

What to Do:

1. Center and ground.
2. Hold the brown jasper between your hands. Say, *"Brown jasper, strengthen my ability to keep up, enhance my endurance, and grant me the ability to absorb and retain the necessary information required for success and release the rest."*
3. Keep the stone with you during study sessions, when working overtime, and in other situations in which you can be overwhelmed by information.

Defense Against Social Media Overload

Social media is a blessing in that it helps you stay in touch with friends and meet people from all over the world, but the flip side is that you are exposed to a constant barrage of disturbing news, arguments, hatred, and causes. Apart from reducing your social media use or limiting the kinds of accounts you follow, try this spell to help protect yourself from the onslaught of emotion that comes with social media use.

What You Need:
Pale blue candle and candleholder

Matches or lighter
Quartz crystal

What to Do:

1. Center and ground.
2. Light the blue candle. Gaze at it and feel the color fill you with calm.
3. Hold up the quartz and unfocus your eyes, gazing at the candle through the stone.
4. Say, *"Quartz, help me sift through the emotion that vibrates in social media. Help me to safely identify what to devote my time and attention to, so that I can safely navigate the Internet without drowning in fear, anger, and pain. Help me resist clickbait, trolling, and guilt trips."*
5. Place the quartz at the base of the candle and let it burn down. Carry the quartz with you or leave it next to wherever you check social media most often.

Defense Against Burnout

Burnout is the physical, mental, or emotional collapse from overwork. It can bring apathy, lack of connection, and a loss of joy in things you used to like doing. Healing from burnout is difficult. Why not use spellwork to help protect yourself against it happening in the first place? This spell uses the symbolism of water to help you go with the flow instead of fighting to hold your ground, which can drain you.

What You Need:
Water

Small bowl or wineglass

Floating tea light candle

Matches or lighter

What to Do:

1. Fill the bowl or wineglass about ⅔ with water.
2. Gently place the floating candle into the water and light it.

3. Say, *"I stay strong. I am balanced. I flow with the tide. My flame burns brightly as I ride the waves. I will not be worn down."*
4. Allow the candle to burn out. Dispose of the remains of the candle and pour out the water outdoors.

See also the Saying No spell in this chapter. Using it can reinforce your ability to handle your schedule by turning down certain tasks.

PROTECTING YOURSELF EMOTIONALLY

Emotional health is just as important as physical health. The term *heartsick* isn't just poetic affectation. Your emotions can have impact on your physical and mental health. Protecting your emotional energy from being drained is an essential part of magical hygiene. Defending your emotional energy from being leeched or drained by others is also important. The more you defend your own energy, the better able you are to help others when they need it.

Protection from the Past

Your past defines you, whether you like it or not. Things that happened to you as a child, as a young adult, even yesterday have an effect on the choices you make and the person you are today. However, some of those things that affect you are unhealthy and hold you back. Living in the shadow of your past can hobble you and render you incapable of fully living in the present. Release these negative things with this spell and start clearing away the unhealthy ties that bind you and prevent you from fully living your life today.

What You Need:
String, about 10 inches long   Blue lace agate
Scissors

What to Do:

1. Center and ground.
2. Hold the string by the ends, stretching it out taut in front of you. Say, *"I am not bound by the negativity in my past. I free myself of its constraints."*
3. Release one end of the string so that it hangs down. Use the scissors to cut the string in half.
4. Pick up the blue lace agate stone. Hold it first against your forehead, then against your heart. Say, *"I release you, weights that drag me down. I release you, fears and sadness. I release you, past. I move forward freely."*
5. Bury the string outside. Carry the blue lace agate with you or keep it somewhere safe.

Healthy Heart

Self-love is extremely important. Your heart is worthy of protection!

What You Need:

Rose quartz   Small wooden box

Dried rose petals

What to Do:

1. Cleanse the rose quartz according to your preferred technique from Chapter 7.
2. Center and ground.
3. Hold the rose quartz between your hands. Clasp it to your heart. Say, *"This rose quartz is my heart."*
4. Place the rose petals in the wooden box. Place the rose quartz on the rose petals. Say, *"My heart is my own; it is safe from attack, safe from pain, safe from abuse."*
5. Keep the wooden box in a safe place.

Sometimes you can find heart-shaped rose quartz stones. One of those would be ideal to use for this spell.

Protected Heart

Defend your heart's energy from being drained by other people. Even if you allow someone into your heart, letting them drain your heart's energy is detrimental to your relationship. You need to be able to function healthily in order to participate in an equal relationship. Of course there will be times when one of you has to be the strong one and give to the one in pain, but if your partner drains you without thought to your well-being and does it frequently, then you need to take action to defend yourself.

What You Need:
Quartz crystal point
Silver chain, such as for a necklace

What to Do:

1. Center and ground.
2. Hold the crystal in your hands, saying, *"This quartz is my heart, this quartz is my spirit. It holds infinite energy. It is my reservoir, a source of energy from which to replenish myself when I require."*
3. Wrap the silver chain around the quartz, tying it in place. Say, *"Thus do I secure my energy, my spirit. It is mine; no one may take it without my permission. At no time will anyone drain me; the quartz is a deep pool of energy. It is always available to me. No one else may take its energy."*
4. Keep the chain-wrapped quartz somewhere safe in your house or room.

A quartz crystal point is a longish piece of quartz rather than a tumbled stone, usually with a rough point on one end. You can use a crystal rod as well for this spell if that's easier to find. The chain doesn't have to be pure silver; it's just symbolic.

After a Breakup

Be it a romantic breakup or the loss of a friend after an argument, magic can help you soothe a troubled heart and release pain. Allowing the relationship to be released allows you to move on. This spell can be performed during the separation process or afterward.

What You Need:
Handful of salt

What to Do:

1. Go to a moving body of water: for example, a lake, a pond, a stream, or a river.
2. Center and ground.
3. Hold the salt in your hand. Pour your emotions about the situation into the salt: disappointment, anger, sadness, confusion. Send whatever energy you wish to release concerning the relationship into the salt as well.
4. Say, *"I release you,"* and toss the salt into the water.

General Emotional Negativity Defense

This is a very simple spell that can be performed daily. It absorbs the emotional negativity around you and reduces the amount that gets past it to affect you.

What You Need:

White cotton thread or lightweight yarn
Scissors
Heatproof dish
Matches or lighter

What to Do:

1. Center and ground.
2. Cut a length of the cotton yarn about 10 inches long. Tie it into a loop and slip it over your wrist.
3. Say, *"White cotton, absorb the general negativity around me so that my emotional balance remains unaffected."*
4. Wear the loop bracelet all day. At night, slip it off and coil it in the heatproof dish. Say, *"Thank you for protecting my emotional well-being."* Light it and let it and the emotional negativity it has collected burn away.

TIP

- You can use thread for this instead of a lightweight yarn; just make sure it's pure cotton so it will burn properly.

CHAPTER 3:
HOUSE AND HOME

The spiritual identity of your home is formed of its own energies (building, colors, furniture placement, and so forth), the energies of all those living in it (including animals such as pets), the energies of the land it's on, and the surrounding neighborhood energies. Keeping these as positive as possible just makes sense. The house is your safe space. Or it should be! So work to make it as pure and nourishing as possible.

PROTECTING YOUR HOME

Why do you defend a house? To stop break-ins, sure, but also because negative energy gets stuck to things. That negative energy can function like oxidation—rust settling on the bright, shiny parts of the energy of your home. Scrub off that rust. Better yet, wipe down the shiny parts regularly, and the rust won't form, leaving the energy of your home supportive, clean, and positive for everyone in it.

To *purify* (or sometimes to *cleanse*) something means to remove or transform the negative or undesired energy from it. *Cleansing* is more often used to describe the physical level of transformation, while *purification* can refer to the energy state; they are used interchangeably here unless specified because the physical state impacts the energy of an object or space. (A cluttered room often has a very different energy than the tidy version, for example.) Cleansing and blessing are at the heart of all magical maintenance for protective purposes. Once the negative or undesired energy has been cleared, the next step is to fill it intentionally with a specified energy. This is often called a *blessing*, in which positive energy is requested to surround the object or space. Otherwise, nature abhors a vacuum, and any kind of energy will move in to take its place. By being in control of what kind of energy goes into it, you can fine-tune your home's energy to your needs or desires.

ISSUES TO CONSIDER

When working to protect a home, there are a few specific things to keep in mind, and most of them have to do with ethics.

There are ethical boundaries to consider when you work to defend a home. You do have to consider your own safety and wellness, but often, there are other people living in that home with you. As you've seen by working through the earlier parts of this book, everything is connected by energy, and if you tweak the energy of one element, that change is going to ripple and impact all the other energies in the area. Namely, your housemates.

In Part 1, the responsibilities of parents and pet owners were raised. Essentially, as a parent or guardian, you are legally responsible for the minors in your care and therefore make decisions regarding their welfare. The decisions you make about protecting your house and magical maintenance of its energy will impact them. Ideally, everything you do will be to benefit the household.

Ethically, it's also important to remember that your actions will have an effect on housemates as well. You don't have the same sort of responsibility for other adults; in fact, making decisions for others is generally considered infringing on their rights to free will and self-determination. Altering the energy of a home will affect them and how they live in it. Keep that in mind as you work to magically cleanse and protect your home and remember that you're striving to have a safe, balanced, harmonious home.

BE CONSIDERATE OF YOUR HOUSEMATES

Since your primary purpose is removing negativity so that more doesn't come calling, similar to using a mop to clean the floor, your spellwork should generally benefit the household. If you're doing something more substantial that is going to drastically change the energy, it's thoughtful to mention it to your housemates or even to ask their opinions in advance. It can be as simple as saying, "Hey, I'm going to do a little something to deal with that part of the house none of us like to go into because it creeps us out. You okay with that?" You could even ask if they want to help.

GOOD NEIGHBORS

A good neighbor tries not to interfere with or inconvenience those who live nearby. However, there's also a saying that good fences make for good neighbors. When you do magic on your property, make sure it stops at your boundaries. Your neighbors' property is their own, and you have no right to interfere with it.

Unfortunately, some neighbors don't follow the same rules or are not as considerate. Noise, negativity, and other irritants can drift over to your property from theirs. Remember, you have no right to use magic to stop them; what you do have is the right to defend yourself from being impacted by them. Raise those magical fences!

LEARN MORE

For more information on sensing energy and working with it, please see my book *Power Spellcraft for Life.*

MAGICAL MAINTENANCE

The more familiar you are with the baseline energy of your home, the easier keeping it healthy will be. Being tuned in to minor changes will help you head off problems before they become critical. To do that, you need to become adept at evaluating the energy of your home. How do you do that?

Sensing energy is different for everyone, but looking at the most common method(s) will help if you've never worked at something like this before. *Sensing* is a good word for it because it doesn't prescribe what sense you use to perceive or interact with the energy. If asked, most people would say they "feel" energy, which again doesn't prescribe or limit what sense is being used.

Here's a simple exercise to practice sensing energy.

Sensing Energy Exercise

This exercise helps you explore your own methods of sensing energy, an invaluable skill to have when you are working to protect a home. Have a notebook and pen or pencil on hand to make notes as you go; this is part of recording your spellwork as addressed in Chapter 1.

In most of the spells in this book, you can choose to cast a circle or not, as per your personal preference. In this exercise, however, do cast one; it will help block out distracting energy while you focus on sensing the energies of the items you're working with.

What You Need:

Small dish of salt

Notebook and pen/pencil

Small dish of water

Tea light candle

Matches or lighter

Twig

Small potted plant
 or flower

Clear quartz stone

Rose quartz stone

What to Do:

1. Wash and dry your hands.
2. Cast a protective circle (see Chapter 1).
3. Center and ground.
4. Shake your hands as if shaking water off them. Take three deep breaths.
5. Gently hold your hands above the dish of salt. Imagine the energy that flows through your body reaching out to touch the energy of the salt. How does it feel? Does it create a physical sensation? Does it remind you of anything or trigger a memory? Does it alter your emotional state? Do you just feel different in an undefinable way? Is it better or worse?

6. After giving yourself time to explore the energy of the salt with the energy of your hands, gently lower your hands so your fingers physically touch the salt. Does your sense of the salt's energy change at all?

7. After exploring the salt's energy, remove your hands, brush them off lightly, and shake your hands again to help rest and refresh them and rid them of any clinging energy. Take a moment to write down your impressions of the salt's energy.

8. Repeat these steps with the water, the candle (hold your hands to either side of it instead of above it and don't touch the flame), the twig, the potted plant or flower, the clear quartz, and the rose quartz. Make notes each time and shake out your hands. If you need to take a break at any time, do so. Remember that you have a circle up, though, and don't wander through it. If you need to, separate the energy of the circle as if you're opening curtains, step through, then let it fall shut behind you again. Repeat to reenter the circle.

9. When you have finished your exercise, take a moment to center and ground again. Bring down the circle, then stretch to settle yourself firmly in the physical world again. Have a drink of water or eat something.

The two kinds of quartz are there to experiment with how your sensing might differentiate between two similar stones. These are the two most common quartzes used in protection magic and magical maintenance.

Surveying the Energy of Your Home

In this exercise, you're going to visit each room of your house and note what you sense. In this way, you'll familiarize yourself with how things are currently, and when you check later, you can refer to your notes and verify if anything has changed that might need to be addressed. This can be a long exercise if you have a large home; take breaks as you need to, to sip some water or munch some fruit before going on. This can be a tiring task if you're not used to focusing on energy, so don't push yourself too hard.

What You Need:

Notebook or magical journal
Pen or pencil

What to Do:

1. Choose a place to begin. The front door (or whichever door is most frequently used) is a good place to start. Start a new page in your magical journal and date it, then jot a few words down about the exercise's intention. Note the time, the weather, and anything else you want to keep track of. (Is there anyone else in the house? That might be a good thing to note.)
2. Center and ground. If you currently have a personal basic shield up, lower it. If you are concerned about lowering it completely, reduce the density.
3. Extend some of your personal energy out into the room you are in. Open yourself to impressions received from it. How does the room make you feel? Does it have an emotional impact? A mental impact? A physical effect of some kind? Does it remind you of something or somewhere else? Note it in your journal.
4. Move around in the room. Does the energy change at all? Is there more of something in one place, less of it in others? Is there an area of the room that feels particularly comfortable or makes you uneasy? Make notes in your journal. Don't forget to look up toward the ceiling and down into corners.
5. Is there something missing from the room? Does it feel unbalanced somehow? What do you think might help redress that imbalance? Write those ideas down as well.

6. Move to the next room and repeat the process, writing everything down. Continue throughout the house in this way. Don't forget the bathroom, attic and/or basement, storage rooms, and any other rooms you may not frequent on a regular basis.

7. If you have large hallways or corridors, treat those as separate rooms.

8. When you are done, center and ground again, then stretch. Make yourself a cup of tea or drink something cold and eat something to help reseat yourself in the physical world. Then review your notes. Underline or highlight key words in them, a few for each room, as you come across them.

9. This research will be your base reference material for any alternations in your home's energy.

TIPS

- Drawing a map of the room and labeling it with different energy zones might be useful. You could draw a floor plan of the entire house and do the same.

- Study these notes to get a sense of the personality or character of each room. This can also reveal things you hadn't noticed before, like a tendency to lean toward certain kinds of elemental energy (fire energy, for example, can be great for creativity, but it can also trigger confrontations and clashes) that you might want to work to balance out. (See later in this chapter.)

- This is an excellent exercise to do in order to prepare before a full house cleansing/blessing, to determine if you need to focus more on certain areas in the cleansing/purification process. Once the ritual is done, wait a day or so for the energies to settle in place, then redo this exercise to get a feel for the new normal. Doing a house cleansing and blessing is like washing a blackboard clean, starting from scratch at an energy level.

While the earlier exercise on sensing energy had you cast a circle around yourself, that's not going to be as easy in this exercise since you're walking around. You can generally work through this exercise without a shield. However, if you live in a place that has a lot of negative energy, review the Basic Shield exercise in Chapter 2. Remember that you're not trying to block out all energy in this instance because you'll be sensing the ambient energy in the room; just imagine the shield you create to be permeable to the extent that you can "taste" the energy around you but not be wholly swamped by it. Dial down the density of the shield, in other words.

Enchant Cleaning Supplies for Protection

Just like taking your car in for an annual inspection and tune-up is important, regular magical cleansing is a responsible way to maintain the integrity of your home's energy. A home that has good energy hygiene will attract fewer problems, and an ounce of prevention is worth a pound of cure. Magically programming your cleaning supplies is one of the easiest ways to support the magical maintenance of your home. You houseclean on a regular basis anyway, so why not tie magical cleansing into the physical part?

What You Need:
Cleaning supplies (sprays, cleansers, scrub brushes, detergent, rags, and so on)

What to Do:

1. Center and ground.
2. Hold the item in your hands or hold your hands over it. Say, *"[Item], be for me a beacon of brightness, a glow of goodness. Banish any trace of negativity or evil and protect this space. Let it be done!"*
3. Use the item as per the manufacturer's directions.

TIPS

- If you're a fan of making your own cleaning supplies, you can empower them as soon as you mix them.

- You can empower new cleaning supplies as soon as you bring them home and have them ready for use.

- You can refresh this empowerment a few times a year or every time you use the cleaning product. It's up to you. Whatever you feel works best!

Maintenance Survey

This is an exercise to check if you need to renew or beef up your current protections and defenses. "Regular" magical cleansing means different things to everyone. If your home sees a lot of interaction or strangers or tends toward a heavy energy due to its location or the personalities of the residents, then you're going to want to touch up or recharge your protections more often. You can set regular times to purify, or you can do it on an as-needed basis. This exercise will help you figure out if it's time.

What You Need:
Magical journal

Pen or pencil

What to Do:

1. Review the notes you made during your initial energy survey of your house. Review any notes you took during any subsequent surveys. Start a new page in your magical journal and date it, then jot a few words down about the time, the weather, and anything else you want to keep track of.

2. Center and ground. If you currently have a personal basic shield up, lower it. If you are concerned about lowering it completely, reduce the density.
3. Starting where you began your initial survey, move through your house and sense the energy in each room as outlined in the previous exercise. Pay special attention to the spots where you noted issues or anomalies. Has anything changed? Are things worse? Better? Make notes as you go.
4. When you have finished sensing the energy of each room, center and ground again, have a drink, and eat a snack. Review your notes. If everything is exactly the same, you can probably get away with not running maintenance right away. If things aren't at the baseline they should be, evaluate how far off they are and what kind of spells or rituals you need to do to bring things back into line. (Consult the rest of this chapter for ideas.)

TIP

• The more you do this, the better you'll get at sensing the energy of a room, and you'll be able to tell without a formal survey when something is off somewhere in your house.

What do you do if things are *better* than the last time you ran maintenance? Nothing! Be appreciative. It means things are going well.

Seasonal Energy Maintenance

This maintenance spell is set to be performed every full moon, but you may vary the schedule according to your needs: solstices and equinoxes are great, or the first of every month—whatever schedule works for you. Alternately, perhaps you function best on a regular calendar-type schedule, and planning a regular cleansing on the same date every month will help you keep the rhythm. Choose a time that will work for you and blend into your schedule with the least amount of awkwardness. The point is to do it regularly—as regularly as your space requires and your schedule allows.

What You Need:

Incense (sandalwood, sage, frankincense, or your choice) and censer

Matches or lighter
Dish of water
1 teaspoon salt

What to Do:

1. On the day of the full moon or the day before or following it, gather what you need. Center and ground.
2. Say, *"Negative energy, darkness, distrust, fear, I banish you. By the power of my will, I send you from this place."*
3. Carry the incense in a counterclockwise direction through your house. Step into each room and circulate counterclockwise, waving the incense smoke into corners and past large furniture with your free hand. Visualize the negativity as a murky fog that dissipates as the incense swirls into it. Repeat the words as you move throughout the house if you like.
4. When you reach your starting point, put down the censer. Sprinkle the salt into the water and stir it with your finger, drawing energy up from the ground and down your arm to pass from your finger into the water.
5. Say, *"Safety, luck, health, and abundance, I invite you here. Fill this house with your many blessings. Keep us safe and well."*
6. Carry the dish of salt water through your house in a clockwise direction. Dip your fingers into the water and flick them into the air as you circulate through the rooms. Repeat the words as you move throughout the house if you like.
7. When you reach your starting point, put down the water and say, *"It is done."*

Room-Smudging Spell

If you find a particularly icky area in your home during a maintenance survey, if you've just hosted a guest who was extremely aggressive or otherwise negative, or if there's just been a big argument in your home, smudging can help eliminate any residual negativity.

What You Need:
Smudge stick
Matches or lighter
Heatproof bowl

What to Do:

1. Light the end of the smudge stick. Gently blow out the flame once the dried herbal matter has caught. You may hold the smudge stick in your hand for this and hold the bowl underneath to catch any embers or ashes or lay it in the heatproof dish and hold the dish itself.
2. Say, *"Negativity, I banish you; the purifying energy of this sage smudge repels you. Let only harmony and purity remain."*
3. Waft the smoke around the space that needs to be cleansed of negative energy. Extinguish the smudge stick.
4. Allow the smoke to stay for a few minutes, then open a window or turn on the ventilation to help clear the room. Visualize the negativity dissipating with the sage smoke.

TIPS

- Burning sage has a strong smell. You may need to make sure the room is ventilated ahead of time; a smudge stick can create a lot of thick smoke. Less can be more when smudging!
- Smudge sticks come in several varieties. There are different kinds of sage (all of them purify and cleanse) and blends with other herbs like lavender and cedar. Choose whichever one appeals to you.

- You don't have to use an entire smudge stick. Extinguish it by tamping it out in a heatproof bowl or sand. When it's cool, wrap it in foil and keep it till the next time you need it.
- This spell could also be performed with a sweetgrass braid.

Smudging is a quick and easy way to banish negative energy or rebalance things that have gone out of whack. Review the information on smudging in Chapter 2.

Purifying Spray

Water is a very useful element. Cleaning is frequently done with water, and a spray is an easy way to break up negativity in your house.

What You Need:

1 teaspoon dried rosemary
Mug
¼ cup boiling water
Coffee filter or fine sieve
Small spray bottle

Distilled water
3 drops sandalwood oil
3 drops lemon oil (juice may
    be substituted)
Pinch of salt

What to Do:

1. Place the dried rosemary in the mug and pour the boiling water over it. Allow it to infuse for 5 minutes, then strain it through the filter or sieve into the spray bottle.
2. Fill the spray bottle with the distilled water.
3. Add the sandalwood oil, the lemon oil, and the salt. Screw the top back onto the spray bottle and shake it to combine all the ingredients.
4. Set the spray bottle to a fine mist and spray it into the air in the middle of a room. Don't spray it directly on furniture; you don't

want to drench or saturate anything. Just let the fine mist settle and spread its energies.

5. Use as needed to help disperse negative energy.

TIP

* Store this in the fridge to avoid any mold. Replace the solution every month.

Blessed Water

Blessed or holy water is a concept found in many cultures. Water is considered a powerful, transformative thing, and there are many folk practices that enhance it. For example, dropping something made of pure silver into a cup of water would bless it; if the holy water was to be used for healing, gold was sometimes used instead for its connection to the sun. Herbs were also commonly used to enhance the water. This spell uses St. John's wort, which is used to bless both people and houses.

What You Need:
¼ cup distilled water
Glass jar with lid
1 teaspoon St. John's wort
Tea ball or infuser

What to Do:

1. Center and ground.
2. Pour the water into the jar. Place the St. John's wort into the tea ball or infuser and place it in the water.
3. Hold your hands over the jar and say, *"Herb of earth, bless this creature of water, that it may share in your protection and healing. Let it be so."*

4. Place the jar on a windowsill where sun or moonlight (or both) can touch it. Keep it there for a full 24 hours.
5. Withdraw the tea ball or infuser and screw on the lid. Keep the jar in the fridge.
6. Use the Blessed Water to sprinkle on objects you would like to purify or protect, as anointing liquid for yourself, or add a bit to your bathwater.

TIPS

- In a tight spot, use water with a pinch of salt added; that's the simplest Blessed Water you can make.

- Experiment with catching rainwater or using a bowl of melted snow to make Blessed Water.

Uses for Blessed Water

Blessed Water can serve as the basis for several expanded or enhanced spells or potions. You can tweak or enhance certain energies by adding various ingredients or putting the Blessed Water through an extra step to further support your purpose or goal. (Also, as a reminder, you shouldn't drink any version of Blessed Water given here.) Here are a few suggestions:

- Charge the Blessed Water with a specific intent by praying, reciting affirmations, and visualizing your goal and/or the purpose of the water while making it.

- Pour the Blessed Water into a silver-colored bowl (such as aluminum or stainless steel) and place it outside on a full-moon night to absorb the lunar energy. If you don't have somewhere safe you can leave it without worrying that animals may drink from it, leave it on a windowsill inside.

- Make herbal elixirs by steeping herbs in Blessed Water for a few days. Strain the resulting liquid through a coffee filter or cheese-cloth into a jar, cap it, and put it in the fridge. Use quickly because it won't keep long; only make a small amount at a time.

- Add a drop of essential oil to the Blessed Water, such as sandal-wood, rose, frankincense, or lemon.

- Make a stone elixir by steeping any one of the protective stones listed in Chapter 7 in Blessed Water.

Four Thieves Vinegar

Four Thieves Vinegar is a traditional herbal vinegar said to be used by thieves who operated during a medieval plague. When captured, the thieves offered to trade the recipe for the vinegar they claimed had kept them healthy for their freedom. The recipes vary. Here's one that's easy to make. Use it to wipe down a sickroom or to anoint doors and windows to prevent illness from entering.

What You Need:

Jar or bottle with lid or cap

2 cups red wine or apple cider vinegar

2 tablespoons dried rosemary

2 tablespoons dried sage

2 tablespoons dried rue

2 tablespoons dried lavender

2 tablespoons dried mint

9 cloves

What to Do:

1. Ground and center.
2. Pour the vinegar into the jar. Add the herbs. Cap the jar and swirl or shake gently.
3. Allow the vinegar to steep for at least 7 days, swirling or shaking it gently every couple of days.

4. To use, pour some of the vinegar into a bucket of warm water and mop the floor to remove negative energy or dip a cloth into it and wipe down doors and window frames.

TIP

- You can use Four Thieves Vinegar to anoint candles used in protection spells as well, or in spells to turn away evil.

Florida Water

Florida Water is an American version of the French eau de cologne, used to relieve headaches, facilitate relaxation, clear the mind, and scent clothes and linens. Florida Water has an alcohol base, as most perfumes do, and uses essential oils.

What You Need:

Bottle with cap or cork or glass jar with lid
1 cup vodka or other alcohol
3 teaspoons orange flower water
3 drops lemon essential oil
3 drops rosemary essential oil

3 drops lavender essential oil
3 drops rose essential oil
2 drops bergamot essential oil
1 drop sage essential oil
1 drop neroli essential oil

What to Do:

1. Center and ground.
2. Pour the alcohol into the bottle or jar. Add the orange flower water and essential oils.
3. Cap and swirl or shake gently to combine.
4. To use, add a few drops to water and then mist over your body, sofa, or bed linen. Alternatively, add to a bucket of warm water

and mop your floors or dip a cloth into it and wipe down your furniture. (Test a hidden spot first to make sure it will not damage the finish.)

TIPS

- Add a couple drops of Florida Water to your Blessed Water.

- Add a few drops to the water you use to cleanse your stones of unwanted energy.

- You can also rub a bit of Florida Water on your hands after a nasty encounter or a situation with negative people to remove the unwanted energy from your body.

GENERAL HOUSE PROTECTION

Your home is your castle, and it should be defended. Short of a moat, archers on the battlements, and a friendly dragon roaming the area watching for unfriendly attackers, what can you do to protect it?

UNWANTED BUT NOT BAD

Note that in some places energy is referred to as *unwanted*, not as *negative*. There are times when an energy is positive but not wanted in a specific place. For example, energy that soothes and promotes sleep is a positive kind of energy, but it's not desirable in a home office where you want to be alert and productive.

Himmelsbrief

Himmelsbrief literally means "heaven's letter" in German, and is a written letter of prayer for protection. Set versions have been handed down, but creating your own carries the magic of your will, your specific need, and your energy. They can be decorated with images supporting your goal. You can use the spell here or write your own. The key to written magic is to focus on your goal as you craft your piece so it is imbued with your energy and intent.

Himmelsbriefs were used in many different ways. They were hidden in houses when they were built or framed and hung on walls; there were even versions written to protect people instead of homes, which were carried on their persons. This version is one you can hang on the wall. Use your imagination for this one: make a scrapbook page, a collage, use fabric paint...wherever your creative direction takes you!

What You Need:

Scrap paper for drafting your letter

Blank paper, at least 5 inches × 7 inches (color your choice)

Pen or pencil

Ruler, paints, markers, colored pencils, stickers, photos, images (optional; see instructions)

Frame (sized to fit the paper)

What to Do:

1. Plan out your Himmelsbrief using the scrap paper. You can use the written spell that follows or decide what to write, how to phrase it, how to lay it out on the paper, and how to illustrate it.
2. Center and ground. As this will be an extended working, cast a basic circle (see Chapter 1) in which to create your Himmelsbrief.
3. Transfer your layout to your Himmelsbrief paper. In the section reserved for your written spell, write the following (or use the spell you wrote yourself):

By the power of the universe around me,
The sky above me,
The earth below me,
Let no ill will or distress breach these walls.
Let this house be a place of safety, of comfort,
In the names of the honored elements
Earth, air, fire, and water.

4. Illustrate or decorate the rest of your paper as you desire.
5. Bring down your circle.
6. Allow your piece time to dry if necessary. Place it in the frame and hang it in an appropriate place.

TIPS

- While magical work has traditionally been done by hand to infuse as much personal energy into it as possible, in this day and age, there's no reason why you can't make a digital Himmelsbrief and print it out. Or you could display it in a digital photo frame. Use your imagination!

- If this spell appeals to you, use a variation of it to create small protective or evocative collages or artwork for each room in your house.

Similar written protections appear in Hindu and Islamic practice. A modern way to incorporate this kind of protection magic in your home is to design it on your computer, print it on fabric transfer paper, iron it onto a piece of material, and sew it into something such as a pillow or blanket.

Simple House Blessing

Welcome mats, wooden signs that say something about happiness, old-fashioned samplers that say, "Bless this house"…these all have the idea of inviting positive energy into the house. This spell uses a photo, sketch, or other art as a basis for a main blessing for your home. (Do you do needlepoint or embroider? How about wet felting, nuno felting, or needle felting? You could even knit or crochet a small house shape and stuff it!) Don't stress overmuch about creating an exact replica; pick a couple of design features that characterize your house, like gables or your porch, and focus on those and the exterior colors.

What You Need:

Image of your house   4 tea light candles
Dried rose petals   Matches or lighter
Dried lavender

What to Do:

1. Center and ground.
2. Set your house image in the middle of your workspace. Sprinkle the rose petals around it, followed by the lavender.
3. Set a tea light about 2 inches away from each corner of the house image. Light them, saying, *"I call on the energies of the north, the east, the south, and the west to bless this house. Let there be happiness, good health, and good fortune here as long as it stands."*
4. Allow the tea lights to burn out. (This should take approximately 3–4 hours.) Place the image of the house in a place of your choosing. Try to put it in one of the most commonly frequented areas of the house like the living room.
5. Collect the dried rose petals and lavender. You can either sprinkle them outside the house or keep them to add to a house-blessing sachet.

This doesn't need to be a work of art. If you create the image of your house on your own, it will carry the energy you put into creating it. If you're not artistic or don't trust your crafty skills, you can use a photo of your house.

Sympathetic Magic House Protection Spell

Sympathetic magic uses a small representation of the thing you are trying to work magic upon as a focus, using the principle that what is done to the model will also happen to the real thing. This spell uses a mini model of your house. How you construct the model is up to you. You could use clay, Popsicle sticks, LEGO bricks, or anything you like. The bits of physical material from the house can be chips of paint, sawdust from repairs, brick dust scraped from the exterior, or anything along those lines. The idea of incorporating these is to strengthen the tie between the representation and the real-life house.

What You Need:

Material for model of the house
Scraps or bits of the physical building to include
Black silk bag

Pinch of rosemary
Pinch of cinnamon
Black tourmaline
Amethyst
Black ribbon or cord

What to Do:

1. Gather all your supplies.
2. Center and ground. As this will be an extended working, cast a circle (see Chapter 1).
3. Construct the model of your house. As you build it, tuck in the physical bits of the house in whatever way you can.
4. When the model is complete, hold it in your hands and say, *"This is my house; this is my home."*

5. Slide the model into the black silk bag. Sprinkle in the herbs and place the stones in the bag as well. Gather the open end closed and tie it shut with the ribbon or cord. Say, *"My house is safe, my home is safe."*
6. Keep the model in a safe place.

You can sew the black silk bag by folding a rectangle of silk twice as long as it is wide in half so you have a square. Sew along two sides, leaving the third open.

Safe Deposit Box Spell

If you have a safe deposit box, this is a terrific spell with which to protect your home! This is another sympathetic magic spell, in that the representation of your home is used as the focus for the magic that will be transferred to the larger actual house.

What You Need:

Photo or drawing of   Pen or pencil
   your house   Safe deposit box

What to Do:

1. Center and ground.
2. Take the photo or drawing of your house and turn it over. On the back, write the address and the names of the people who live in it.
3. Take the photo to the institution that provides your safe deposit box. When you have been left alone with your safe deposit box, hold the photo in your hands and say, *"This image is my house, this image is my home; it is so."*
4. Place the photo in the box. As you close the lid, say, *"As this document is protected, so, too, is my home protected."* With a finger, draw Othala (see Chapter 7), the rune of inheritance, estate, and family,

on the lid of the box. Lick your finger before drawing the rune to increase the energy you put into it.

5. Allow the box to be returned to the vault.

TIPS

• This is an excellent spell to do with your property deed, if you own your house. In this case, you don't need to write the address on it, and indeed, altering it is not a good idea, as a deed is a legal document. Instead, write out the information on a separate sheet of paper, including the words to speak provided in the spell, and paper clip it to the front of the deed.

• If you rent your home, use your lease for this spell and keep it in a sealed envelope or folder in a filing cabinet or other protected space.

• If you don't have a safe deposit box, you can use a household safe.

Yule Log Spell

If you use a real tree for Christmas, you can incorporate it into an annual protection spell for your house. Pine is associated with purification and protection. Save the part you or the tree merchant cuts off the bottom of the trunk when it's purchased. My family calls this little 1- to 2-inch-thick wooden disk the Yule log. The traditional Yule log is associated with the returning sun and was pulled from the hearth before it was consumed and kept through the year as a talisman against poor health, ill fortune, and danger.

What You Need:
Frankincense and censer
Matches or lighter
The end of a tree trunk, sawed off by the merchant or yourself
Lemon or orange oil (juice may be substituted)

What to Do:

1. Center and ground.
2. Light the incense.
3. Pass the wood through the incense smoke to bless it.
4. Dip your finger in the citrus oil and draw a sun on the cut surface of the wood, saying, *"Yule log, grant us good health and blessings through the year to come. It is done."*
5. Pass the Yule log through the smoke again. Place it somewhere safe near the center of your home for a year.
6. When you next bring a seasonal tree home, dispose of the previous year's Yule log with thanks, by either burning it or adding it to your compost. Repeat the spell with the new cutting from the trunk.

TIP

- If you don't get a tree, you can do this spell with dried pine needles collected from a cutting used as a bough or wreath.

Horseshoes

Horseshoes are a common symbol of good luck. The iron in them repels evil. If you can get one, hang it inside the house over the front door or just opposite it.

What You Need:
Horseshoe
Nails
Hammer

What to Do:
Nail the horseshoe above your front door. Make sure you hang it with the open end facing up; this catches and holds the luck. If you hang it with the open end down, then all your luck is said to drain away.

TIP

- Some traditions reverse the meanings of the horseshoe's position, saying that the open end down pours luck onto your property. Decide which makes the most sense to you and position your horseshoe accordingly.

Blacksmiths are usually the only people allowed to hang a horseshoe upside down, to allow the luck to pour into their forges.

Broom Magic

Of all the magical tools, the broom is the most useful in magical maintenance. No other tool addresses the concept of cleansing so neatly (if you will pardon the pun). Perhaps because of this, the broom has a lot of folklore attached to it. Dedicate your own broom to protecting your house.

What You Need:
Incense (frankincense or sandalwood) and censer
Matches or lighter
New broom
Sharpie marker

What to Do:

1. Center and ground.
2. Light the incense and pass the new broom through the smoke to remove any energy it brought into the house with it.
3. With the Sharpie, write on the handle "I sweep away negativity" or a similar phrase of your choice. Start near the bristles and spiral the phrase around the handle. When you are finished, say, *"It is done."*

TIPS

- If you prefer, you can carve the words onto the wooden handle of the broom. Use appropriate safety precautions. Pyrography can also be done.

- If you have to dispose of the broom (for example, if the handle breaks or the bristles wear out), thank it before you throw it away. Never bring a broom from one house to another. Throw it out and buy a new one. You don't want to bring the negative stuff from one place to another.

- It's also unlucky to borrow a broom because you risk bringing unknown or undesired energy into your home.

> You can use any broom, but one with a wooden handle and straw bristles will carry a more natural energy, which will better support your magic.

New Year's Spell

Use your broom to sweep away negative energy at New Year (either Samhain or the new calendar year). This is another folk tradition that is found in several cultures. Start the new year with a clean slate for your home and reduce the chances that bad luck or negativity will carry over into the new year. Do this at sundown or at midnight.

What You Need:
Broom

What to Do:

1. Center and ground.
2. Starting at the front door, begin to sweep your floor while visualizing all the anger, stress, pain, and sadness of the past year being

gathered up by the bristles. Go back and forth, moving gradually toward the back door of your house.

3. When you have swept the whole house and have reached the back door, open the door and sweep out the bad luck and stale energy. Shake the broom out. Close the door, then go to the front door and open it to allow the positive energy and potential of the new year to flow into your freshly swept space. Say, *"Welcome, new year. Bring your blessings and good fortune to this household. Let it be so!"*

TIP

- If you like, you can pass the broom through purifying incense again after a large job like this. See the previous spell for a refresher on how to do that.

Quick Good Morning Spell

This is a quick way to refresh the energy of the house first thing in the morning. It's a nice thing to do to start your day while your coffee is brewing or your tea is steeping.

What You Need:
Broom

What to Do:
Take your broom and sweep the house, visualizing any stale or negative energy dissipating as you sweep, leaving behind fresh, sparkling energy. If you like, you can say something like, *"I welcome the new day. May the universe grant me strength and keep me safe and well."*

Sweeping Powder

Need a little bit of something to break up the energy before you sweep? This powder is laid down before you sweep an area and absorbs or neutralizes the negativity.

What You Need:

Mortar and pestle

Handful of salt

1 tablespoon sage

1 tablespoon rosemary

1 tablespoon cinnamon

Broom

Dustpan

What to Do:

1. Center and ground.
2. Place all the ingredients in the mortar. With the pestle, grind them until they are finer. They don't absolutely need to be reduced to a fine powder, but do grind them enough to make the herbal matter smaller. If your mortar is small, you may need to do each ingredient separately and then combine them.
3. Carry the mortar to the room(s) you wish to sweep and sprinkle pinches of the powder on the floor.
4. Leave the powder on the floor for at least an hour; overnight is ideal.
5. Use your broom to sweep up the powder, collecting it in the dustpan. When you are done, flush the contents of the dustpan down the toilet.

TIPS

- Instead of a mortar and pestle, you could blend the ingredients in a blender to reduce them to a powder.
- If you have leftover powder, you may store it in a small container for next time. Make sure to label it with the contents and date.

Onion and Lemon Purification

Sometimes there's just one spot in your house that needs attention. This is another simple folk practice.

What You Need:
½ lemon or onion
Small bowl or saucer

What to Do:
Place the lemon or onion in the bowl or saucer and place it in the room that needs negativity or other unwanted energy cleared. Leave it there for 3 days, then dispose of the produce off your property.

TIPS

- If the negativity is really bad, place half a lemon or onion in each corner of the room.
- If you have pets, only use lemon. Onions are toxic to dogs and cats.

Stone Protection Spell

Using crystals or stones to clean or maintain an area is an easy way to manage the energy of a room or house.

What You Need:
Clear quartz crystal

What to Do:

1. Cleanse the stone per your preferred method from Chapter 7.
2. Center and ground.
3. Hold the stone in your hands and say, *"Crystal, be for me a guard against negativity. Defend this room against ill will, misfortune, and conflict."*

4. Place the stone somewhere either central to the room or in a place where it can "see" as much of the room as possible; the edge of a higher bookshelf might be good. If your doorframe is deep enough, you might be able to set it on the lintel right above the door.
5. Remember to cleanse this stone regularly since you have charged it to deflect negativity.

TIP

- If you have a room that needs heavy protection from negative energy, use four crystals, one in each corner.

Entrance Blessing

The *Carmina Gadelica* is a collection of Scottish folk prayers, incantations, blessings, and poems collected from Scotland between 1860 and 1909. It's an amazing collection of oral tradition, full of texts that can be used for prayer or spellwork. This spell uses one of those texts as written magic.

What You Need:
Paper (a blank index card is fine)
Pen or pencil
Thumbtack (or other method of fastening the card to the wall)

What to Do:

1. Center and ground.
2. On the index card, write out the house blessing from the *Carmina Gadelica*:

God bless the house,
From site to stay,
From beam to wall,
From end to end,

From ridge to basement,
From balk to roof-tree,
From found to summit,
Found and summit.

3. Pin or otherwise fasten the card above the front door.

Welcome Mat Spell

Everyone passes over a welcome mat on the way into your home! It's an ideal object to use in magic designed to protect your home. For suggestions regarding other symbols of protection, consult Part 3.

What You Need:
Welcome mat
Sharpie marker

What to Do:

1. Center and ground.
2. Turn the welcome mat over. With the Sharpie, draw Othala (see Chapter 7), the rune of family and estate, and any other symbols you choose to use.
3. When the marker is dry, flip the mat over and place it in front of your door, saying, *"Defend this home; delay and defer those who wish us harm. It is so!"*

TIP

• If you prefer, you can alter this spell to bless anyone who crosses your threshold.

Room Guardian Spell

If you feel a room needs very specific protection, try creating a room guardian for it. This spell invites the energy of an animal, mythological creature, saint, or deity that resonates with you to guard your space, using a representation of the entity as a focus. That representation can be a statue, a photo, a painting—anything at all. For ideas, look at the lists in Part 3.

What You Need:

Frankincense and censer

Matches or lighter

Image of your chosen
  guardian

4 tea light candles and
  holders

Dragon's blood incense and
  censer

What to Do:

1. Center and ground.
2. Light the frankincense. Take the representation of the entity you have chosen to protect the room and pass it through the incense smoke, saying, *"I cleanse this image of any negative or unwanted energy."* Set the image down in the middle of your workspace. At this point, you may extinguish the frankincense or move it to another room.
3. Light the four candles and place them around the image. Light the dragon's blood incense.
4. Hold your hands over the image and say, *"[Name the image], I invite you to bestow your protection upon this space. May it be safe under your guardianship, free from threat and danger. May all who use this room know the benefits of your shelter."*
5. Allow the incense and candles to burn out.
6. Place the image in a suitable location, such as by a door, on a shelf, or on a table central to the space.
7. Make sure to thank your guardian regularly. Tie it into your regular maintenance of the energy in the room, for example.

Instead of choosing the entity to be a protector, you can meditate and ask the universe to reveal a protector who volunteers to work with you to guard the room. You might end up with something you never considered but that works very well.

PROTECTING YOUR DOORS AND WINDOWS

Doors and windows sometimes receive specific protection as they are passages and orifices that allow movement into and out of your home. Sealing them magically can bring you peace of mind.

Magical Symbols

One of the easiest ways to protect doors and windows is to draw protective symbols on or above them. Grab a white crayon and check the list of protective symbols in Chapter 7 to find one that resonates with you. Or design your own; remember, the more input and energy that comes from you, the stronger your magic will be.

What You Need:
White crayon

What to Do:

1. Center and ground.
2. Using the white crayon, draw your chosen symbol above the windows and on or above the door. Don't press too hard; the idea is to have the image be barely visible.
3. As you draw each, say, *"I charge you to defend this home; none shall breach this [door or window], none shall enter with malicious intent. This [door or window] shall not fail or fall; it has the strength of a mighty wall. It is done!"*

TIPS

- If you prefer, draw an image of an animal you associate with defense and protection instead.

- Remember to scrub the images off if you need to repaint because the wax will repel the paint. You can redraw the images after the new paint has dried.

- If using a wax crayon concerns you, use chalk instead, in a color that matches your paint color.

Seal Windows

Windows are clear, allowing the passage of light. However, the permeability and transparency of glass means people can also perceive them as being vulnerable to the passage of energy as well, specifically negative energy. There is a vulnerability to transparency. This spell magically seals the windows to prevent negative energy from passing through.

What You Need:
Blessed Water (see spell earlier in this chapter) or holy water
Small paintbrush with fine tip (optional; see instructions)

What to Do:

1. Ground and center.
2. Dip your finger or the paintbrush in the Blessed Water. In the center of the window, draw a small circle. Paint an X within that circle, saying, *"This window is sealed; no unwanted energy shall enter, no misfortune pass through. It is closed to evil; only good shall pass in. It is done!"*
3. If your window has multiple panes, draw the symbol in the center of each.

TIPS

- If it resonates better with you, draw a single diagonal stroke from the upper left to lower right across the circle to recreate the familiar "do not" symbol found on products and signage that forbids certain actions or behaviors.

- The energy and intent is what counts here, so if you wash your windows the protection remains. However, if you feel the need to redo this spell after you've washed the windows for extra security, go ahead.

- For more permanent protection, charge a bottle of clear nail polish with protection and use it to paint your chosen symbols on the glass.

Mirror Spell to Deflect Negativity

Mirrors and shiny reflective surfaces have been used in magic for centuries to deflect and reflect unwanted energy. This spell enchants a mirror to reflect negativity right back out the front door. If you buy a new mirror for this spell, make sure all tags and labels have been removed and cleanse it according to your preferred method from Chapter 7.

What You Need:

Small decorative mirror
Soft cloth
Blessed Water (see spell in
    this chapter)

Sharpie marker
Hook or nail
Hammer

What to Do:

1. Center and ground.
2. Use the cloth to wipe down the mirror so it is free of dust. Shake out the cloth.

3. Dip the cloth in the Blessed Water and wipe down the front of the mirror, saying, *"Mirror bright, mirror strong, protect this house all day long. Mirror strong, mirror bright, protect this home all through the night."*

4. Turn the mirror over. On the back, write, "Negativity reflects away." (Don't worry if the backing is black. The words will still be there.)

5. Mount the hook or nail in your chosen place across from the door using the hammer and hang the mirror.

TIP

• For extra power, enchant the mirror during a full moon and allow it to remain in the moonlight overnight.

Be extremely precise in your visualization during this spell. You don't want the mirror to reflect good stuff away from your house as well as the bad.

Doorstep Spell

Sometimes protecting the entrance to your home is as easy as this. You can use whatever kind of cooking salt you have: table salt, sea salt, pickling salt, or anything else.

What You Need:
1 teaspoon salt

What to Do:

1. Cup the salt in the palm of your hand. Close your eyes and imagine it glowing with a white light.

2. Say, *"Salt, be my defense. Let no bad fortune or negative energy cross you."*

3. Sprinkle the salt in a line along your doorstep from one side to the other.

TIPS

- Don't worry about drawing an unbroken line with the salt; it's the energy that forms the barrier.

- This is a great spell to do if you feel uneasy.

- If you want to use this spell for ongoing protection, repeat it once a month or once a week if you feel you live in an area with a lot of negative energy.

Lock Spell

You trust the lock on your door to secure your home from those who would unlawfully force entry. It makes sense to add a layer of magical reinforcement to the mechanical security. Cinnamon and ginger are good to add energy or power to something, and caraway possesses excellent anti-theft energy.

What You Need:

Small bowl, jar, or vial
1 tablespoon olive oil
Pinch of powdered cinnamon
Pinch of powdered ginger
Pinch of caraway (powdered is ideal, but seeds are fine)

What to Do:

1. Place the oil in the bowl. Add the herbs and swirl to combine. Allow to sit for at least 1 hour, ideally overnight.
2. When ready to perform the spell, bring the bowl to the door. Center and ground.

3. Dip your finger in the oil and draw a circle around the lock on both the outside and the inside. Say,

Lock, be strong.
Resist any unauthorized entry,
Block those who would do harm,
Lock, be strong.
If someone bears a stolen key, lock,
Deny them access.
Lock, be strong;
Lock, defend.

4. Repeat on any other outside doors with locks that you have, including outbuildings and gates.

TIPS

- You can rework this spell so the lock never jams for someone who legitimately holds a key.
- You can also use this spell on your car doors and ignition.

PROTECTING SEPARATE ROOMS

You may find that certain rooms in your house respond better to specific techniques. That's fine. Use the technique that works best in the room you're purifying. It may be a bit more work to switch techniques if you're doing a full house purification, but in the long run, it's best for the overall energy of the home. The point is to be as effective and efficient as possible, and while changing techniques may take a bit more time, it promotes a smoother household, which in turn affects everything done inside it.

Kitchen Protection

Rooster and witch symbols have been popular in kitchens to attract abundance and good luck. Another item often seen is a rope of braided garlic or onions. It's not just for decoration; these two vegetables from the allium family are both strongly associated with protection.

What You Need:

Braid of onions or garlic (purchased from a farmers' market)

Hook or nail and hammer (optional; see instructions)

What to Do:

1. Center and ground.
2. Hold the braid and say, *"You are charged to keep this house safe from harm. Bless this kitchen, and let no ill luck descend upon it. May the food created here be blessed; may those who cook and eat here be blessed. It is done!"*
3. Hang the braid in your chosen area; install a hook or nail if there isn't a convenient place to hang it.
4. Allow it to hang all year and take it down with thanks for its work at the next harvest time. Compost the old braid and replace it with a new one.

TIPS

- This spell calls for an already-prepared braid, which you can find at farmers' markets around harvest time, but if you want to make one with onions or garlic that you grow yourself or harvest elsewhere, you can find simple instructions online at www.theartofdoingstuff .com/how-to-braid-garlic-or-onionsphoto-video-tutorial.

- You can sometimes find colorful braids of hot peppers as well. Hot peppers are used to return evil to the sender and work equally well in this spell.

Warning: do *not* eat the vegetables from a braid designated to protect! The vegetables absorb negative energy as part of their purpose; that's not the kind of energy you want to consume.

Candle Spell for Protection 1

Candle magic is easy to do. The components are easy to find, and the magic is quiet and not showy; the candle can be burned with other people being none the wiser. Choose a candle in a color you associate with protection for this spell. This spell uses a pointy object to inscribe words on the candle. There is an actual tool for this, known as a burin, but the easiest thing at hand will probably be a metal or bamboo skewer in a kitchen drawer. You can even use a cheap ballpoint stick pen in a pinch.

What You Need:

Candle (white or color of
    your choice)
Skewer or long nail

Candleholder
Matches or lighter

What to Do:

1. Center and ground.
2. Starting at the bottom of the candle and spiraling around to the top, write, "This room is protected" over and over until you reach the top. Finish the phrase; you may have to change the angle of your spiral to fit the last words in near the wick. (You don't need to do a tight spiral and cover every inch of the candle with words; a loose spiral will suffice.)
3. Set the candle in the candleholder. Light the candle and say, *"As this candle burns down, the shield rises. This room is protected."*
4. Allow the candle to burn down completely.

TIPS

- This spell is a good all-purpose protection spell. You can adapt it to protect just about anything.

- Using small candles shortens the time you need to wait before the spell is complete.

Candle Spell for Neutralizing a Threat

This is a great example of how you can tweak a spell and turn it around to address the problem from another direction. Black is a good candle color for this one.

What You Need:

Candle (black or color of
　your choice)
Skewer or long nail

Candleholder
Matches or lighter

What to Do:

1. Center and ground.
2. Starting at the top of the candle and spiraling around to the bottom, write, "The threat is removed" over and over until you reach the bottom. Finish the phrase; you may have to change the angle of your spiral to fit the last words in near the base. (You don't need to do a tight spiral and cover every inch of the candle with words; a loose spiral will suffice.)
3. Set the candle in the candleholder. Light the candle and say, *"As the candle burns down, so, too, does the threat decrease."*
4. Allow the candle to burn down completely.

TIP

- Don't leave a burning candle unattended. If you have to leave before the candle has burned out, gently pinch out the flame. Relight it when you return and allow the candle to burn down completely.

Candle Spell for Protection 2

This slightly more complex spell pulls in the protective and cleansing properties of lemon as well as color and flame.

What You Need:

Small vial or jar

1 teaspoon olive oil

3 drops lemon oil or
     juice

Candle (white or color of
     your choice)

Candleholder

Matches or lighter

What to Do:

1. Mix the olive oil and lemon oil or juice together in the vial.
2. Hold the candle in one hand. Dip the fingers of your other hand in the oil mixture and begin rubbing it onto the candle from the wick end to the base.
3. When the candle has been covered with the oil, place it in the candleholder and say, *"Lemon and fire, neutralize any evil that threatens. Let it be so."*
4. Light the candle and allow it to burn down in a safe place in the room.

Protection Incense

This incense is composed of a selection of herbs associated with protection. To burn it, you will need a charcoal tablet, available at ethnic stores, ecclesiastical supplies stores, and new age shops. Make sure your herbs are dry. Suggested herbs for this spell are angelica, cinnamon, caraway, rue, rosemary, juniper berries, cedar, and dried lemon zest. Most of these herbs are available in your supermarket spice aisle.

What You Need:

1 teaspoon each of three to five herbs, chosen from the suggested herbs
Mortar and pestle or cutting board and knife
Small jar
Charcoal tablet
Matches or lighter
Heatproof dish or censer with a layer of sand or earth in it
Trivet

What to Do:

1. Choose your dried herbs. Place 1 teaspoon of each of them in the mortar and use the pestle to grind them together. If you do not have a mortar and pestle, heap the teaspoonfuls together in the center of the cutting board and mince them finely with the knife.
2. Spoon the powder into the small jar. Hold the jar in your hands and close your eyes. Visualize the powder inside glowing with defensive energy.
3. Take your supplies to the room you wish to defend. Set up in the middle of it.
4. Place the charcoal tablet in the heatproof dish or censer and the dish or censer on the trivet. Hold a flame to the edge of it until red sparks appear along the edge of the tablet. When the tablet catches, the red sparks will begin to travel across it. Once they have stopped, give the charcoal a few minutes to settle.
5. Center and ground.
6. Sprinkle a pinch of the incense powder on the tablet. Smoke will begin to rise. Waft it around the room with a hand, waving the

smoke away from yourself in an outward motion. Say, *"Incense, I call upon your powers of protection. Defend this room; let negativity be barred."*

TIPS

- If any of the herbs you want to use aren't dried, you can dry them in a low oven. See the instructions in Part 3.

- You can put a bit of sand down in a dish or censer to absorb the heat of the charcoal tablet. Fine gravel or non-clumping kitty litter works too. Remember, incense charcoal is *not* barbecue charcoal.

Room Guardian Spell

This spell creates a focal item to protect a specific room. It takes a bit of preparation on your part. Review the maintenance exercises earlier in this chapter and determine what kind of energy focus the room needs. Does it need more loving energy? Does it need active protection? Does it need to encourage harmony? Once you've determined the room's requirements, you must choose a focal object for your magic that resonates with that need. This spell assumes that you have a room that needs support for rest and recuperation, such as a bedroom.

What You Need:

Piece of paper   1 teaspoon dried lavender
Pen or pencil   1 teaspoon dried chamomile
Small statue or figurine of a
    swan

What to Do:

1. Center and ground.
2. On the piece of paper, write words associated with the energy you wish to strengthen in the room. In this case, words such as *sleep,*

calm, *dream*, and *heal* all work. You can repeat the words several times. Don't just make a list; turn the paper and angle the words, making a crisscross weave of written words like a net.

3. Hold the figurine of the swan. Close your eyes and breathe slowly and deeply, as if you were asleep. Relax your body, releasing as much tension as you can. Visualize the swan growing, spreading its wings, sheltering you with them.

4. Say, *"Swan, guard this room. Bless it with peace, rest, healing, and calm."*

5. Place the figurine on the paper. Sprinkle the paper and swan with the dried lavender and chamomile. Allow them to stay there for at least 1 hour.

6. Remove the figurine and place it somewhere in the room where it can extend its protection and blessings. Fold the dried flowers up in the paper and compost them.

TIP

• Match the object that you choose as the focus for your room with herbs that support its goals. For example, if you want to guard a room where you work, you could use an image of Thoth, the Egyptian god of writers and wisdom, and pair it with dried mint and bay leaves, both associated with mental work and inspiration.

Water Spell to Absorb Negativity

Water is used in some cultural traditions to absorb negativity. Here's a simple way to cleanse negativity from a room.

What You Need:
Glass or dish
Water

What to Do:

1. Fill the glass or dish with water.
2. Center and ground. Hold the dish or glass in your hands and visualize it glowing with a pale blue light. Say, *"Let all negativity in this room be absorbed by this water. Water, I thank you for your transformative energies."*
3. Place the dish or glass somewhere it won't be knocked over that is central enough to be within the flow of energy in the room. The water will absorb unwanted negativity.
4. Replace weekly if the room is a low-negativity area or daily for maximum protection.

Salt Dough Charm

Did you build things with homemade modeling dough when you were a child? The basic salt dough recipe makes a terrific base for a protective charm. Salt has excellent protective properties, as do rosemary, sage, and lavender. Note: use inexpensive table salt for this project, not fancy or chunky salt. The dried herbs can be ground or crumbled; just don't use fresh.

What You Need:

½ cup flour
¼ cup salt
Small mixing bowl
Wooden spoon
¼ cup water
1 teaspoon rosemary
1 teaspoon sage

1 teaspoon lavender
Cookie cutter (optional)
Foil pie pan or sheet of foil
    and baking sheet
Chopstick
String

What to Do:

1. Stir the flour and salt together in the small mixing bowl with the wooden spoon. Stir in the dried herbs. Add the water very slowly, stirring it in. (You may not need all the water.)
2. Knead the dough on a lightly floured surface for 8–10 minutes.
3. Let the dough rest for 30 minutes.
4. Preheat the oven to 250°F.
5. Roll the dough into 1½-inch balls and flatten them gently with the palm of your hand to about ¼ inch thick. Alternatively, roll the dough out on a lightly floured surface and use a cookie cutter to cut out shapes.
6. Use a spatula to transfer the shapes to a foil pie pan or a foil-lined baking sheet. Use the larger end of the chopstick to make holes in the shapes with which to hang the charms.
7. If you wish, use the narrower end of the chopstick to draw a protective symbol on the shapes.
8. Place the pan or sheet in the oven and bake for about 4 hours. You can flip the shapes over after 2 hours to dry the shapes thoroughly. If your shapes are thicker than ¼ inch, it may take longer than 4 hours; keep an eye on them and check often.
9. Remove the shapes from the oven and allow them to cool. Thread a piece of string through the hole and hang each charm wherever you feel it's needed.

TIPS

- If you use a cookie cutter, circles and stars make excellent protective shapes.
- How many shapes a cookie cutter will make depends on the size of the cookie cutter; the balls will make four to six shapes.

PROTECTING YOUR PROPERTY

Sometimes your neighbors aren't as easy to get along with as you wish they were. Sometimes you want a little bit of extra defense in your neighborhood because of the amount of traffic through it or the location. And sometimes, you just want to keep yourself to yourself. Whatever your reason, defending the property that is defined as yours is your right, and if you consider yourself to be a steward or custodian of the land, protecting it is also a duty. If you rent, you can still work to protect the land around the building you live in.

The following spells focus on the outdoor portion of your home.

General Property Protection Spell

This spell uses the same principle that your basic personal shield does (see Chapter 2). Instead of standing in the center, pulling the energy up from the ground, and pushing it out on a sphere, however, you're going to actually walk around the perimeter of the property (as best you can), drawing a line of energy as you go. Start at a place that makes sense to you, such as the gate.

What to Do:

1. Center and ground.
2. Keep drawing energy up from the ground. Allow it to flow down your arms to your hands. Point a hand at the ground and begin to walk around the edge of the yard, visualizing the earth energy flowing out into a ribbon.
3. As you walk, say, *"This land is protected. None may harm it. No evil may cross this barrier."*
4. Complete the circuit around the yard. Visualize the energy ribbon meeting the original end and sealing together to make a seamless ring encircling the yard.

5. Visualize the circle of energy sinking into the ground. Repeat, *"This land is protected. None may harm it. No evil may cross this barrier. It is done."*

TIPS

- If you can't walk all the way around your property because of fences or other obstacles, do this in two (or more if necessary) separate stages, front and back.

- If you have obstacles that prevent you from actually walking the very edge of the property, such as a shed or freestanding garage, raise your arm to project the energy and visualize sending it behind the obstacle.

- For extra protection, bury cleansed and charged stones at the four corners (or cardinal points) of the property. Malachite is a good stone for this as it's associated with protecting the environment.

Beating the Bounds

Believed to be derived from pagan roots, this ancient custom is still observed in areas of Britain and Wales. The term refers to beating or pounding the perimeter of your property with a branch to break up negative energy and bless the land. This practice also delineates and reinforces your protective energy boundary as well as allowing you to check over the physical status of the property. Spring is the ideal season to do this spell.

What You Need:
Pitcher of water   Long branch or stick

What to Do:

1. Set the pitcher at your starting point.
2. Center and ground.

3. Start swishing the branch or stick back and forth beside you as you walk around the perimeter of your property, striking the ground. As you do, say, *"Waken, earth, from your slumber! The sun shines, the air beckons; bestir yourself! May you receive that which is sown, may your growing season be healthy, may your harvest be plentiful. I banish the negative energies that threaten you; begone, misfortune, and never return."*
4. When you finish your circuit, put down the branch and pick up the pitcher of water. Pour it on the ground where you began and ended your circuit, saying, *"I thank you, earth, for your many blessings."*

TIP

• If talking while you walk is hard to do, whether because you have difficulty holding a book or paper and handling the tools at the same time or you need to watch where you're going, you can speak the words of the spell at the beginning before you start walking and again at the end when you've completed your walk.

PROTECTING YOUR GARDEN

If you are a gardener, protecting your plants and produce is always a concern. This section covers defending your garden as well as using your garden to defend the property and home.

Tree Spell for Protection

One of the most rewarding ways to protect a property is to plant a new shrub or tree. It is a gift to the land as well as the environment in general. Check your city or state for programs that distribute free or low-priced saplings for Earth Day, Arbor Day, or other similar occasions. Choose your area for planting carefully; make sure it's not too close to buildings so the roots don't damage water systems and the branches don't interfere with power lines. Your city may have laws regarding how close to property lines a tree may be planted.

The following sidebar lists some trees and shrubs and their magical properties. Choose one from there or go with whatever is offered to you. Look up the properties of that tree and tweak this spell to include those correspondences. In the end, it's the tree itself that is important, not its specific magical energies. Trees represent stability and strength, both things that tie in well to protection.

What You Need:

Shovel	Black earth
Quartz crystal	Hose or bucket of water/
Sapling	watering can

What to Do:

1. Dig the hole for your sapling. You should have received a leaflet or information sheet along with your tree, but if you didn't, research it online and note the information. A good guideline concerning hole size is to allow the existing root system plenty of room to spread out, both horizontally and vertically. The diameter of the hole should be two to three times the width of the root ball. The hole should be just slightly deeper than the height of the root ball; the top roots should be level with or just below the surface of the soil.

2. Place the quartz crystal in the bottom of the hole, saying, *"Earth, be kind; help this tree to grow. Protect it from disease and danger, so that it in turn may protect us."*

3. Set the sapling in the hole. Have a friend hold it straight while you fill in the hole with the earth you dug out. Add black earth to help refresh the earth you moved. Don't pack it down; roots need air and loosely piled earth so they can grow properly. This also ensures proper water drainage.

4. Set the hose on the hole and run the water slowly, allowing it to soak into the area for at least a couple of hours. Water the tree

every day for at least a month, paying attention to the weather in your area to adjust the amount appropriately.

TIPS

- If you don't have room for a tree, why not a fruit bush? Blackberry canes are said to magically keep unwanted influences away from your property.

- Having a second pair of hands to help with this is useful. Otherwise, use a pole to help prop the sapling up; tie it carefully with twine if you need to.

Here is a small selection of trees and shrubs and their magical properties: *apple*: abundance, health; *ash*: protection; *birch*: children, purification, protection; *hawthorn*: protection, happiness; *lilac*: protection, love, purification; *juniper*: cleansing, purification, protection; *rose*: love, purification, blessing, positive energy; *oak*: strength, protection; *pine*: healing, purification; *rowan*: protection, blessing; and *willow*: protection, healing.

Rune Stone Garden Spell

Planning and digging a new garden is an exciting project. This spell blesses and protects a newly made or prepared garden bed.

What You Need:

4 smooth river stones or
    pebbles
Long nail
Trowel

Watering can with Blessed
    Water (see sidebar)

What to Do:

1. Center and ground.
2. With the nail, scratch one of the following runes on each stone:

- Othala: Ancestors, guard this land and property.

- Ingwaz: May this garden be fertile.

- Algiz: May this garden be defended.

- Jera: May this garden yield successful harvests.

3. At each corner of the bed, dig a hole with the trowel. Put one stone in each hole and cover them up.
4. Take the watering can and say, *"Blessed earth, may you be defended from disease and barrenness. May your crops be fruitful and many; may your yields be abundant. It is so!"* Sprinkle the garden with the Blessed Water.

> In the case of gardens, Blessed Water or holy water can't be made with salt, as salt is bad for green growing things. Instead, try making it by dropping something silver, a quartz, or a malachite stone into the water. See earlier in this chapter for how to make Blessed Water.

SPECIFIC SPELLS FOR APARTMENTS AND CONDOS

If you live in a temporary home, something you don't own, what can you do to protect it? Rentals, townhouses, apartments, or shared buildings are a challenge; your space is right up against someone else's. The previous section on ethics is applicable here as well. If you live in a shared building, there are the rights of others to consider. Your magic must therefore be focused specifically on you and your personal space.

Likewise, anything more permanent or long lasting that you do to the structure or space must be *undone* when you leave.

Moving Out Spell

Living in a space means your energy soaks into the walls. Loving, laughing, and mourning in a place means your energy is attached to it, and your energies are entwined. This is great if you want to be able to effectively and easily modify the energy of your home…but not so great if you have to move out. This spell is designed to help you extricate yourself from the energy of your dwelling, leaving you and the place separate entities again.

What You Need:
Incense (frankincense or sandalwood) and censer
Matches or lighter

What to Do:

1. Center and ground in the middle of the living space.
2. Light the incense. Say, *"Respected house, thank you for your years of shelter. Release to me the energies that are mine, that I may take them with me when I go and not trouble you. I leave you purified and ready for your next tenant."*
3. Close your eyes and hold out your arms. Visualize your energy slowly being drawn toward you from all over the house, floating to your hands, where it is absorbed. Channel that energy up your arms and to your core and from there down your connection to the ground and the energy of the earth.
4. Allow the incense to burn out.

TIP

- You can use a sage smudge for this instead if you prefer.

This spell has you do the reverse of grounding, in which you draw energy up from the ground. Here you will be drawing energy from elsewhere and shunting it down to the ground so you do not hold too much energy inside you; it allows you to equalize safely instead of overloading.

Spell to Create a Home Guardian

As in the previous spell, you can certainly weave spells and protection into the walls of even a home that doesn't belong to you, as long as you make sure to withdraw, dispel, or otherwise unplug them when you leave. However, a good alternative to enchanting a permanent structure is to enchant a painting, statue, or other moveable object to be the protector of your home, wherever that may be.

What You Need:

Malachite

Smoky quartz

Tiger's eye

Item to be the focus (e.g., statue, painting)

1 teaspoon dried rosemary

1 teaspoon dried sage

1 teaspoon salt

Tea light candle

Matches or lighter

Small blue pouch

What to Do:

1. Prior to the spell, cleanse the stones and object you have chosen to be the focus according to your preferred method (see Chapter 7).
2. Center and ground.

3. Sprinkle the rosemary, sage, and salt in the center of your workspace. With your finger, draw the Eihwaz rune (see Chapter 7) in the herbs. Place the focus for the spell on top of the rune.
4. Place the malachite slightly behind and to the left of the focus. Place the smoky quartz behind and to the right of it. Finally, place the tiger's eye in front, between you and the focus. The stones should mark the points of an inverted triangle, with the focus in the center of it.
5. Place the tea light in front of the tiger's eye and light it.
6. Hold your hands over the setup. From your energy center, reach down through your connection to the earth to its energy and draw some up. Bring it down through your arms to radiate from your hands and energize the focus. As you do, say, *"I invoke the spirit of home. I invoke comfort and safety; I invoke peace and harmony; I invoke strength and resilience. Spirit of home, I gather you here, in this focus. May those who live within your care prosper; may they be healthy, strong, brave, and stable. Let it be so!"*
7. Step back and shake your hands free of any excess energy. Remember to consciously stop actively drawing up energy through your connection to the earth.
8. Allow the candle to burn out. When it has, collect the herbs and stones and slip them into the small blue pouch. Place the focus and the pouch somewhere in the main room of your home.

The stones in this spell are all chosen to offset the potential negative effects of many people living in close quarters in a place like a dormitory or school residence, an apartment block, or a row of townhouses. Malachite works to ease environmental stress, tiger's eye offers you strength, and smoky quartz absorbs negative energy.

CHAPTER 4:

FAMILY AND FRIENDS

Protecting people dear to your heart is usually a primary concern. This chapter explores ways to do that. However, protecting others falls within the tricky ethical gray area. If someone calls for good thoughts or prayers about a situation they're involved in, that's a green light. Go for it. However, oftentimes things are not so clear.

If you see friends in difficult situations and want to help magically, the most obvious thing to do is to ask their permission to do spellwork on their behalf. If they're okay with it, you're set. They may want to set limits or ask you to focus on a specific aspect of their case; that's their right. If they refuse or if you cannot ask them for whatever reason, then you need to consider your options.

Instead of working magic aimed at a person in particular, you could try working to improve the situation, leaving the mode of improvement vague enough that the energy will make its own decisions. Consider adding a line to your spell that allows the person's own energy to reject whatever energy you are stirring; this allows him or her to have agency, even subconsciously.

It's a thorny problem. Only you can decide what is right. Know, however, that you accept the consequences of whatever you take on.

PROTECTING INDIVIDUALS

Helping people is part of what spellwork is about. Sometimes that person is you; sometimes it's a friend. This section of spells looks at helping people who are not necessarily family, although they can certainly be used for family members as well. They look at helping people regain control of what's going on in their lives. The spells aren't cure-alls, nor do they assume you know better than the individual you are working to support. Remember, though, if you're working for someone specific, it's still best to ask for his or her permission.

General Protection Spell

This spell sends good stuff to everyone—no one in particular singled out, no specific situation or issue pinpointed. It's a nice blanket good-vibes kind of spell, and it can make you feel pretty good too. The world could use some good vibes in general, don't you think?

What You Need:

Blue candle and candle-
    holder
Rose quartz

4 obsidians
Matches or lighter
1 teaspoon salt

What to Do:

1. Center and ground.
2. Set the blue candle in the holder at the center of your workspace. Place the rose quartz at the base of the candle. Place one obsidian at each corner of an imaginary square around the candle and stone.
3. Light the candle, saying, *"May those people I know who are in my heart be protected; may they be safe from harm, from danger, and from misfortune. May blessings brighten every part of their lives. Let it be so."*
4. Carefully sprinkle the salt in a circle around the setup. Allow the candle to burn down.

Ice Spell

Sometimes the situation a friend or loved one is in is so bad that you need to slow it down or put it on hold for him or her. This spell helps give the person time or space to think things through or make a plan.

What You Need:

Slip of paper
Pen or pencil
Small freezer-safe container
    with lid
Water
Freezer

What to Do:

1. Center and ground.
2. Write the situation out on the piece of paper. For example, if your spouse is having a tense time at work, write something like "Jim's stressful office situation."
3. Fold the paper and put it in the container. Pour water over it, just enough to cover it. Snap the lid on.
4. Place the container in the freezer and allow the water to freeze.
5. You can keep this spell active for 7–10 days maximum. When it's time, remove the container from the freezer and allow the ice to melt.
6. Center and ground. Say, *"I release this situation. May resolution ensue, to the best possible outcome. Let it be so."*
7. Pour the water outside. Compost the wet paper or bury it.

TIPS

- This also works with a small zip-top bag instead of a container.
- Try using this spell to freeze anxiety about an upcoming event or activity.

This is not a permanent spell; it's a temporary pause, no more. After about a week, you're going to have to take the container out of the freezer and allow the ice to melt. If you don't, the situation is going to gather steam again on its own. It's better to remain in control of how the spell is released.

Ice Spell for Unblocking

This is the reverse of the previous spell; this takes an ice cube and uses it as a symbol for an obstacle that's blocking someone. Before you begin, think up a short phrase that describes the situation, such as "The runaround and lack of resolution to Kathy's insurance appeal."

What You Need:
Bowl
Ice cube

What to Do:

1. Center and ground.
2. Place the ice cube in the bowl. Hold the bowl and say, *"I name you [situation]. Melt, melt, and unfreeze the processes by which resolution must be found."*
3. As the ice cube melts, visualize it releasing the energies required to get the situation moving toward a resolution.
4. When the ice cube has melted, say, *"It is done."* Pour the water outside.

TIP

- This spell can also be used to remove personal obstacles, like writer's block or fear about an upcoming event.

BFF Support Spell

When separated, things once united or paired can be used as a connection between them. A BFF necklace can become the basis for a mutual protection spell, assuming the two people involved are okay with that. It's a nice way to reinforce an existing deep friendship, especially if you live in different cities and don't see each other very much. It's a way to keep an eye on each other and support each other even if you can't be there in person.

Beware: if your friend is going through a hard time, this spell could draw on your own energy to help him or her through. It can also serve as a wordless communication; it may alert you to your friend's need for support or contact and vice versa.

What You Need:

Photograph of your friend or a possession of his/hers
2 candles (white, blue, or gold) and holders

BFF necklace set
2 quartz crystals
2 rose quartz crystals
Matches or lighter

What to Do:

1. Place the photo of your friend in the center of your workspace. Place the two candles in the holders behind it. Place the BFF necklace below the photograph. To one side, place one clear quartz and one rose quartz; put the other clear quartz and rose quartz on the other side of the photo. Light the candles.
2. Center and ground.
3. Hold your hands over the photo, necklace, and stones. Say,

   Be my strength, as I am yours,
   Let our friendship support us in times of need,
   I am there for you as you are there for me.

4. Allow the candles to burn down.
5. Give one rose quartz, one clear quartz, and one half of the pendant to your friend. Keep the others.

TIP

*   If you don't want to wear the pendant as a necklace, attach it to your keychain, a bracelet, or your work lanyard…you have lots of options!

Note that this spell requires two people who are okay with being linked like this.

FAMILY

Family is a very special case. Protecting your family is a generational impetus, a natural instinct. The thought of your family members being vulnerable to danger is deep and visceral, and the intense fear of being unable to protect them is terrifying.

Using spellwork to protect family and support all the other work you do to keep them healthy, safe, and happy is an extra layer of security. It can provide comfort for them, as well as for you.

Spell to Invoke Ancestors to Protect You and Your Family

Protecting the family relationship and strengthening the familial bond are key elements of defending your loved ones. One way of doing this is by honoring your ancestors and inviting them to bless their descendants. Be aware that by doing this, you are formally recognizing your ancestors and their place your life. Ignoring them afterward is likely to undermine your request for help!

What You Need:

Frankincense or your preferred incense and censer
Matches or lighter
White pillar candle (or vigil candle or other jar candle)

What to Do:

1. Center and ground.
2. Light the incense. Spend a moment or two in reflection, thinking about your ancestors.
3. Light the pillar candle, saying,

   Respected ancestors of our hearts, of our bodies, of our spirits,
   You who have brought us here,
   Who lived, loved, and laughed,
   Who fought for justice, who shepherded the innocent,
   We honor you here now.
   We thank you for the lives you lived
   And ask that you bless us.
   Guard us as we live our lives,
   And protect us from those who would do us wrong.
   Let it be so.

4. Allow the candle to burn for a while until the incense burns out. Then extinguish the candle and put it in a safe place.
5. Once every 2 weeks (or every month or whatever regular schedule feels appropriate), relight the candle and repeat the ancestor invocation.

TIP

- This can be a nice thing to do as a family. Family members can take turns reading the invocation.

Unlike other spells in this book, this spell calls for a pillar candle because it should be relit periodically to honor your ancestors.

Spell to Anchor a Safe Family Space

Spellwork can also strengthen the family unit by enhancing the environment in which its members interact. By working to create a safe space in which to engage, you can promote safety, trust, and closeness.

What You Need:
One stone/crystal per family member (see following sidebar)
Small glass bowl
Family photo

What to Do:

1. Cleanse the stones beforehand according to your preferred method from Chapter 7.
2. Center and ground.
3. Hold each stone in turn and think about the person in your family whom it represents. Then place it in the bowl and say, *"Our family exists in a safe, loving, supportive space. Communication is clear and calm."* If you are doing this spell with your family, each person holds his or her own stone and says the words as he or she places it in the bowl.
4. Place the family photo on top and say, *"It is so."* If your family is with you, everyone can say it at the same time.
5. Put the bowl somewhere central to where the family gathers most frequently, such as the dining room or living room.

TIP

• A Mini Witches' Ladder (see Chapter 2) makes a great addition to this spell. Coil it and put it in the bowl or fasten the ends together to make a loop and place the bowl inside the circle.

This spell calls for one stone per family member. You can ask each family member to choose his or her own stone or select one for each of them based on how you perceive them.

Spell to Support Family Communication

One of the most common places a family gathers is at the dining table. It's where food is shared, conversation and planning take place, and work is done. Empowering it for clear communication and love is a terrific way to add a level of protection to the family's bond.

What You Need:
Blessed Water (see Chapter 3)
Clean cloth

What to Do:

1. Center and ground.
2. Dampen the cloth with the Blessed Water and wipe down the table, saying,

   Let this table be a place of comfort.
   May it serve as a place to learn, to support,
   And to share.
   May the communication around it be clear, respectful,
   And loving at all times.
   It is done.

TIP

- This is something that can be repeated regularly at a frequency of your choice or according to how often you feel it needs to be done, such as weekly or once a month.

Enchant Kitchen Tools for Safety and Health

Of course you want your family to be healthy and happy. Apart from making sure your knives are kept sharp (which reduces the chance of accidents), safety in the kitchen is a practical sort of protection to support with magic. This spell focuses on knives, but you can use it as a template for other tools as well.

What You Need:
Kitchen knife or knives

What to Do:

1. Center and ground.
2. Hold the knife in your hand. Draw energy up from the ground and let it flow down your arm to the knife. Say, *"Knife, tool of my hand, cut safely, cut cleanly."*
3. Repeat with the rest of your knives.

TIP

- Use this format to bless other tools in your kitchen. For example: *"Spoon, tool of my hand, blend smoothly, blend well."*

New Year's Eve Spell

If your family has had a bad year and you're not the kind of person who carefully saves the family wall calendar every year as a souvenir or record, you can burn the old calendar to prevent bad stuff from carrying over to the new year. If you don't want to burn the calendar itself, take time to sit with the calendar and go through it page by page, writing down the bad stuff—the car repairs, the trips to the ER, the arguments—and burn the paper you write them on instead.

What You Need:

Calendar of the year just ending

Large heatproof container (see sidebar)

Matches or lighter

Bucket of sand or pitcher of water

What to Do:

1. Center and ground.
2. Hold the calendar and say, *"Begone, negativity! Ill fortune and sickness, I command you to disappear. Remain in the past and haunt us no more. It is so!"*
3. Tear the pages from the calendar one by one. Drop them into the heatproof container. Light the edges of several and allow the flames to spread. Depending on the kind of paper the calendar is printed on, the flames may catch quickly, or it may take some work to establish them. Be determined!
4. Keep watch over the fire until all the paper is consumed. When there are only embers or ashes left, pour the sand or water on top to extinguish it completely.

TIP

- When you start your new calendar, keep a parallel tiny notebook or a dollar-store agenda to write these things down in, then burn that at the end of the year. You can start doing this anytime during the year. It's never too late.

If you have one, a fireplace or fire pit is ideal for this spell. If you do not, a large cauldron or cast-iron Dutch oven on a heatproof surface such as bricks or paving stones will serve. If you don't have a fireplace, perform this spell outside.

New Year Calendar Spell

This spell empowers your new calendar for luck and to attract positive energy. This is designed to be used on the main family calendar, but you can also use it on your pocket agenda, bullet journal, or school agenda. It's best to do this on New Year's Eve or New Year's Day.

What You Need:

New calendar
Dried basil
Dried rose petals
Dried clover flowers

Aventurine
4 tea light candles
Matches or lighter

What to Do:

1. Center and ground.
2. Lay the new calendar in the center of your workspace.
3. Sprinkle the herbs and flowers on top of it. In the center, set the aventurine. About an inch away from each corner of the calendar, set a tea light.
4. Light the tea lights, then say, *"Let this coming year be blessed with good luck, good health, laughter, joy, and success. It is so!"*
5. Allow the tea lights to burn down. When they are finished, sweep up the herbs (compost them), remove the aventurine, and hang the new calendar up.

TIP

- You don't need to save the aventurine. Cleanse it and put it back in your box or bag of stones to be used in future spells.

First Day of School Spell

This was originally designed in tandem with a child who was terrified of his first day of school. It can be adapted for any age and for the first day of any anxiety-inducing undertaking. The idea is to invoke things that make you feel strong and successful. If you're doing this for a child, have him or her participate with you. The child's input is key to the spell's success. Let him or her use whatever colors he or she likes.

What You Need:

Paper

Scissors

Pen, pencil, or crayons/
colored pencils

At least one thing that gives
you strength (such as an
animal or creature)

Three positive words

Rune or symbol

Small pouch or sachet

Penny from your birth year
(or another coin from
that year)

What to Do:

1. Cut the paper into smaller pieces. You can cut one letter-sized sheet into four (4-inch × 5-inch) pieces.
2. On one piece of paper, draw a picture of at least one animal or creature that makes you feel strong and safe.
3. On another piece of paper, write three words that describe how you want to feel at school. Words like *safe*, *happy*, *brave*, *smart*, and *strong* work well for this. If you're working with a child, let him or her decide.
4. Choose a symbol that is associated with protection (see Part 3 for ideas) and draw it on another slip of paper. Again, if working with a child, let him or her choose; the symbol may not be traditional but may have deep meaning to the child. Captain America's shield, Wonder Woman's eagle symbol, the Transformers symbol…these

are pop culture symbols that can carry great meaning for a child. Roll with it.

5. Fold up the papers small enough to fit in the pouch or sachet. Name each thing as you slip the paper into the bag. For example, *"I am protected by the wolf and the unicorn. At school I am smart, brave, and strong."*

6. Slip the coin from your birth year into the bag and close it. Say, *"With this bag, I am strong and safe."*

7. Take the bag with you in a pocket when you go to the event or activity you're dreading.

TIPS

- In Japanese culture, charms called *omamori* can be purchased at shrines. These are often made of cloth and look like tags or small bags, sometimes containing a written prayer or blessing. They can be tied to a backpack, schoolbag, or purse and carried for good luck and spiritual protection. This spell is similar.

- When the spell bag is no longer needed, open it and dispose of the contents with ceremony and thanks.

Separation Anxiety Spell

This was originally designed for a child going to preschool for the first time who was nervous about leaving her parents behind. This is a great spell to use if you have social anxiety at any age.

What You Need:
2 matching necklaces, pendants, or bracelets

What to Do:

1. Ground and center.
2. If the child is with you, each of you hold one of the focus objects in your hands. If not, hold both together in your hands.

3. Say, *"My love travels with you today. When I see this, I think of you; when you see this, think of me. We are strong and brave, together and apart."*
4. Place one of each item around the neck (or wrist) of parent and child. (If you're doing this spell for yourself, wear one and loop the other around a symbol of safety and comfort at home—a teddy bear, a photo of you happy and confident, whatever works for you.)
5. Every time you or the child starts to panic, put your hand around the necklace or touch the bracelet and close your eyes. Take three deep breaths, visualizing the other necklace you are connected to as well, secure and safe with someone you love. Remind yourself of how secure you feel there and draw that feeling into yourself so you are brave.

TIP

• Check to make sure a necklace is permitted wherever your child is going. Some schools and institutions don't allow jewelry out of concerns for safety. In that case, draw matching symbols on the back of your hand and your child's hand. Refresh them daily. Or use temporary tattoos.

If this spell is for a child, choose the necklaces/pendants/bracelets together. It's important that the child has input in this; the energy will resonate and flow better if he or she has a personal connection to the item he or she is wearing as a focus.

Protection from Nightmares

Part of taking care of a family means making sure everyone gets adequate quality sleep. Nightmares or disturbed sleep can be a problem. Citrine is a form of yellow quartz that is helpful in defending sleepers from nightmares and soothing physical stress. Lavender is also good for relieving physical stress and for peaceful rest. Together, they make a good team for quiet nights.

What You Need:
Citrine

Small white drawstring bag or square of white cloth and white yarn or ribbon

1 teaspoon dried lavender flowers

What to Do:

1. Ground and center.
2. Hold the citrine in your hand and say, *"Stone so bright, nightmares are banished by your light."* Slip it into the bag.
3. Hold the lavender flowers in your hand and say, *"Lavender, bring peaceful sleep, calm and deep."* Pour them into the bag.
4. Tie the bag closed. Say, *"By this charm, sweet sleep is called."*
5. Tuck the bag under the pillow, hang it on a bedpost, or slip it under the bed.

SPELLS FOR (AND WITH) CHILDREN

Include your children in creating these if you can. They need a sense of power and control over themselves and their environment. Their input is a powerful magic.

STRESS RELIEF
Teaching kids to center and ground gives them a useful skill. It can offer them a moment to find their footing and reestablish their confidence in situations that catch them off balance. It's also a great way to deal with stress.

Child's Spell for Fears

Sit with your children and design a spell with them! This spell revolves around making up an imaginary friend who protects them. It will be particularly powerful for them because they have control over designing their protector.

What You Need:

Paper   Crayons

What to Do:

1. Center and ground. Lead your child through the centering and grounding process as well.
2. Tell your child he's going to design the perfect protector. Ask him what it might be able to do. Would it be tall or tiny? Would it be loud or gentle? Would it be silent or invisible? How many legs would it have? Would it have a tail? What would it do if it saw he was scared? Would it have fur, feathers, scales?
3. Allow the child to imagine whatever he likes. He may get really into it and design several protectors, or he may be uncomfortable and not feel like designing one at all. If the latter happens, end the spell session and try again after he's had a few days to think about it.
4. Have the child draw his protector and name it. Remind him that he can call on this protector to support him when he's feeling nervous or frightened, and it will be there for him.

TIP

• If your child already has an imaginary friend, build on that.

You are the best judge of your child's personality and can present this in the most appropriate way. Tweak it as you need to.

Rhyme to Repeat When Scared

There's something comforting about speaking in a rhythmic pattern, especially when you're stressed. It creates a reliable beat to follow, and a familiar memorized poem or rhyme allows your mind to follow a set path as well. This is a form of word magic. This spell can be tied into the previous spell if the concept of a protective imaginary friend works for your child. If not, it can be used on its own.

What to Do:
Say the following with your child:

One, two, three,
Nothing harms me.
Four, five, six,
No mean tricks.
Seven, eight, nine,
All is fine.
Count to ten,
Everything's zen.

Anti-Bullying Spell

Bullying can have a significant impact on a child's psyche. Intimidation is a difficult force to counter, especially when a child may already worry that she is on the weaker side of a power imbalance. Help a child strengthen her sense of personal power by giving her a charm bag to carry.

What You Need:
Obsidian
Tiger's eye
Red jasper
Brown jasper
Blue candle and holder
Matches or lighter
Blue bag or pouch (or the child's preferred color may be substituted)

What to Do:

1. Cleanse the stones according to your preferred method from Chapter 7.
2. Center and ground.
3. Light the candle.
4. Pick up the obsidian, saying, *"Obsidian, shield against negativity."* Place it in the pouch.
5. Pick up the tiger's eye, saying, *"Tiger's eye, protect from physical harm and strengthen courage."* Place it in the pouch.
6. Pick up the red jasper, saying, *"Red jasper, support justice, defend against physical threat."* Place it in the pouch.
7. Pick up the brown jasper, saying, *"Brown jasper, ensure safety in this ongoing stressful situation."* Place it in the pouch.
8. Close the pouch and say, *"Let this power imbalance right itself. May the truth come out. May justice prevail."*
9. Place the pouch in front of the candle and allow the candle to burn out.
10. Give the pouch to the person feeling bullied.

This spell is for support; it is not a replacement for action! Nothing replaces the child informing a staff member or trusted adult about bullying so it may be dealt with properly.

PROTECTING YOUR PETS

Pets deserve protection and care as well as the human members of the family unit. These spells focus on the furred, feathered, or scaled members of your household.

Pet Collar Protection Spell

If your pet goes outdoors, a collar is a necessity. Some indoor animals wear them as well. This spell uses the collar as the focus for a protection spell.

What You Need:
Pet collar

What to Do:

1. Center and ground.
2. Hold the collar in your hands and say,

   Be a shield for this animal.
   Keep it from harm.
   Encircle it with love and protection
   As long as this collar is worn.
   Let it be so.

3. Buckle the collar around your pet's neck.

TIP

- You can replace the second to last line with *"As long as this animal lives"* if you prefer.

Safe Return Spell

This spell enchants the registration and/or vaccination tags on a pet's collar to encourage a safe return home.

What You Need:
Sheet of paper
Pen or pencil
Registration and/or vaccination tags (on or off the collar)

What to Do:

1. Center and ground.
2. Draw a picture of your house on the piece of paper. It can be a simple shape or outline. Make sure it's big enough so that the tags and/or collar can fit inside the drawing. Write your address inside it.
3. Place the tags and/or the collar on the paper inside the house. Say,

   Home, home, home,
   Return, return, return,
   Safe, safe, safe.

4. Hang the tags on the pet's collar or buckle the entire collar on, repeating the words again.

TIPS

- Repeat this yearly, when the registration is renewed or the vaccinations are updated. Some pets are issued new tags annually, while other tags are permanent and the files renewed. Either way, renewal time is a good reminder to refresh the spell.

- If your pet does get lost, you can use this spell as a focus to help it return home. Place a photo of your pet inside the drawing of your house instead of the tags/collar.

Spell for Good Health

This is a spell on your pet's food bowls and is designed to bestow health and strength on the animals who eat from them.

What You Need:

Pet bowls (or water fountain, water bottle, and so on)

What to Do:

1. Wash and dry the bowls.
2. Center and ground.
3. Hold your hands over the bowls and say,

   May those who eat and drink from these bowls
   Know health, happiness, and joy.
   Grant them long lives and contented hearts.

CHAPTER 5:
OUT AND ABOUT

Protecting your home is well and good, but you spend a lot of time on the road and in other places, like work or school, as well. This chapter covers spellwork that focuses on those other locations.

PROTECTION FROM DANGER

Public danger is a concern that magic can't miraculously remove. Magical protection works on a magical level; that is to say, it works to increase your protection and reduce the chances of negative activity being attracted to you or happening in your presence. It will not, however, completely eliminate the possibility of violence or conflict in a public place.

What can help, however, is strengthening your perception so you can spot a dangerous situation before it becomes too bad to escape. You can also reduce your chances of being targeted for violence by working a "don't see me" kind of spell. In all these kinds of spells, you have to listen to your intuition. If you ignore the warnings your awareness tries to send you, these spells will be pointless.

Augmenting Your Shield

Refer back to Chapter 2 and review the Basic Shield spell before you perform this version.

What to Do:

1. Center and ground.
2. Draw up the earth's energy and form it into a shield around yourself, as in the Basic Shield spell. Don't forget to reach up and form the dome over your head and underneath you as well.
3. Focus on the energy of the shield. Say, *"Shield, I charge you to watch for danger. Alert me when my safety is threatened, that I may remove myself from that danger."*

Sharpening Your Senses

Working to sharpen your senses and fine-tuning your perception can help you in a tricky situation, allowing you to get away before it spirals out of control.

What to Do:

1. Center and ground.
2. Focus your awareness on your body, then carefully reach out that awareness in all directions. Stop about 4 or 5 feet in each direction.
3. Say,

    I have the hearing of the hare,
    The eyes of the hawk,
    The wisdom of the owl.
    As danger approaches,
    I feel it,
    And act accordingly.

4. Be mindful of the messages your senses send you.

TIP

• Remember, when you start working to enhance your senses, there can be an adjustment period when you feel like everything is loud and intrusive. It will pass when you adjust to filtering through the new information you are learning to receive.

Invisibility Spell

While this spell won't completely erase your presence, it will encourage people to look past you, thereby reducing the chance that you could be targeted.

What to Do:

1. Center and ground.
2. Imagine seeing yourself from someone else's viewpoint. Slowly envision your outline blurring and fading so your shape is only a vague outline.
3. Say, *"Blur their sight so I may remain unnoticed. Look past, look past, look past."*

TIPS

- This doesn't actually erase you from people's perception. Any sudden movement or activity outside the expected can and will be noticed.

- Slow movement or movement matching those around you will help you blend in and reduce your chances of being noticed.

PROTECTING YOURSELF DURING TRAVEL

Travel is a tricky thing. It's neither here nor there; it's a transitional experience. This section includes spells to protect yourself while moving from place to place during commuting and short-distance trips as well as on longer journeys.

You can, of course, use any of the general protection spells from Chapter 2 while you travel. Those are good all-purpose spells that can be tweaked to suit a specific travel-related intention. Here, though, are some specific travel-related spells to use.

Visualization Spell for Safe Travel

The easiest thing you can do is visualize a safe journey. All it takes is a minute of your time and focus. This spell has you focus on the positive outcome itself, instead of the journey.

What to Do:

1. Center and ground.
2. Visualize yourself arriving at your destination, calm and carefree. See yourself sitting down and relaxing after the trip, meeting with the people you plan to see. Imagine a conversation with them in which you laugh and say that the trip went off without a hitch. In this way you're training your mind to expect the positive outcome of safe travel. And as like calls to like, you thereby increase your chances of accomplishing that safe journey.

Pennies for Safe Travel Spell

This is a spell that we return to again and again in our house. It's simple, direct, and quick. If you don't have a penny, use any coin you can find from the individual's birth year.

What You Need:

1 penny for each person traveling, from that person's birth year

Tea light candle and holder
Amethyst
Matches or lighter

What to Do:

1. Center and ground.
2. Place the pennies in the tea light holder. Place the tea light on top of them. Place the amethyst in front of the candle.
3. Light the candle and say, *"Spirits of the road, smile upon us. Grant us a safe journey and a safe return."*
4. Allow the candle to burn down halfway, then extinguish it.
5. When you return from your trip, relight the candle and say, *"Spirits of the road, thank you for guarding us as we traveled."* Allow the tea light candle to burn down completely.

TIP

- Keep the pennies handy for other spells involving the family.

Passport Protection

Your passport is your identification and guarantee of freedom of movement between your home and the places in the world you want to visit. Keeping it safe should be of paramount importance to you. Apart from the mundane precautions (such as leaving it in a safe either in your room or at the hotel's desk, making copies of the important pages and leaving one at home while carrying the others in your luggage, carrying the passport in a flat money belt under your clothing), here is a spell to cast before you travel so your passport has an extra layer of protection.

What You Need:

Passport
5 quartz crystals
Bay leaf
Pen or pencil

Gold candle and candle-
   holder
Matches or lighter

What to Do:

1. Center and ground.
2. Set the passport in the center of your workspace. Place a quartz crystal on each corner.
3. Draw the Eihwaz rune (see Chapter 7) on the bay leaf. Place the bay leaf in the center of the passport cover and set the final quartz on top of it.
4. Set the gold candle in the candleholder behind the passport. Light it and say,

    Passport, you are my companion on my journey.
    Keep me safe; be defended from theft.

May my journeys with you be blessed with joy,
And smooth transitions from one place to another without incident.
Allow me to return home safely.
Let it be so.

5. Allow the candle to burn down.

TIP

- You won't be able to bring the bay leaf with you, but you can tuck it inside the passport until you leave, then put it back in when you come home.

Travel Florida Water

Florida Water (see Chapter 3) is a terrific magical all-purpose aid when you're traveling. It can cover several different needs, such as purifying a space like a hotel room, refreshing the interior of a rental car, and helping you ground or clear negative energy by rubbing some on your hands. If you're flying or crossing a border, you probably won't be able to bring your own with you, but it's common enough that you can probably purchase a premade version at a pharmacy or drugstore. If you can't find any or prefer to make your own, here's a quick and easy substitute you can make on the road. It is best refrigerated, or it won't last long.

What You Need:

Small bottle of still water
Clean glass
Slice of lemon
Slice of orange
Few grains of salt
Few drops wine or
other alcohol

What to Do:

1. Center and ground.
2. Open the bottle of water. Pour some into a clean glass.

3. Place the lemon and orange slices into the glass of water. Add the salt and the wine or other alcohol.
4. Swirl gently, then allow it to rest for at least 1 hour, preferably overnight.
5. Remove the slices of fruit. Carefully pour the liquid back into the water bottle. Cap it and swirl to blend. Refrigerate or keep in a cooler if possible. Discard after 4 or 5 days.
6. Use as you would regular Florida Water: sprinkle on objects or in an area, anoint possessions, rub on hands, and so forth.

PROTECTING YOUR VEHICLES

A car, motorcycle, or other vehicle is a big investment. Even if you ride a bike as your main mode of transport, money has gone into it, and you rely on it. Protecting your vehicle(s) is a smart thing to do. This next section features spells that are specifically focused on vehicles.

Visualization Spell for Vehicles

One of the first things you can do when you get in a car or on the seat of a bike is protect yourself with creative visualization. It's quick, direct, and uses nothing but the power of your mind.

What to Do:

1. Center and ground.
2. Close your eyes and visualize a gleaming silvery mist forming in the air around you. Imagine it forming into a cloud of shimmering energy, expanding to encircle your vehicle as well. When you are ready, visualize it melting into the frame of the vehicle itself and/ or your protective gear.

TIP

- This spell can be used when you travel on public transport, trains, and airplanes too.

Talisman for Travel Protection

Talisman bags for protection are often carried on your person or hung near a door, but you can also put the talisman in the glove compartment of your car. If it is small enough, you can hang it from your rearview mirror.

What You Need:

Small square of black fabric,
 at least 6 inches square
3 juniper berries
1 smoky quartz

1 bay leaf
Red ribbon or cord,
 measuring 8–10 inches
 long

What to Do:

1. Center and ground.
2. Spread the cloth flat on your work surface. Place your hands upon it and say, *"Black cloth, protect my vehicle from danger and evils; be active and vigilant."*
3. While visualizing the protective energy gathering, place each herb and the stone in the center of the fabric, saying, *"Into this talisman I place juniper, to guard from evil. Into this talisman I place smoky quartz, to protect from danger. Into this talisman I place bay, to warn me of hazard."*
4. Draw the sides of the fabric up and wrap the red ribbon around it, saying, *"Red ribbon of protection, bind this talisman together."*
5. Tie the talisman shut with three knots, visualizing these knots as barriers to negative influences.

6. Place the talisman bag in the glove compartment of your car, saying, *"My car is safe; my car is protected; those who travel in it shall be delivered securely."*

TIP

- The finished size of this is about 3 inches × 3 inches. If that's too big for a vehicle like a motorcycle or bike, feel free to size it down as far as you can.

Key Chain Amulet

You always travel with keys, whether they be for your vehicle, the workplace, or home. Anxiety about potentially losing your keys is common. This spell works to promote protection during travel and against the loss of the keys.

What You Need:
Leather cord, approximately 10 inches long
3 beads (see following sidebar)
Tea light candle and holder
Matches or lighter
Your keys

What to Do:

1. Center and ground.
2. Thread the beads onto the leather cord and tie the cord in a loop.
3. Place the loop in front of the tea light candle. Light the candle and say, *"Amulet, I charge you to protect my keys; may they never stray, may they never be misplaced. Amulet, I charge you to extend that protection to the car; may it roll safely, may it protect its occupants. Amulet, I charge you to do these things. Let it be so."*

4. Let the candle burn down. When it has, thread the leather through your keychain and tie it off using a squarc/rccf knot (not a granny knot) for security.

TIP

- Trim the loose ends of the loop off if you like.

This amulet is constructed of three wooden or stone beads. Have fun browsing through the beading section of your local craft store looking for beads with colors and patterns that appeal to you. Look for beads about half an inch wide and make sure the holes are large enough to accept the leather cord you plan to use. Red, black, blue, and white are colors associated with protection if you want to include them.

New Tires Spell

A new set of tires is an excellent opportunity for spellwork to enhance their safety and performance. You can also use this spell when you rotate your tires or change them from the winter to the summer set and vice versa.

What You Need:
Tires
White grease pencil

What to Do:

1. Center and ground.
2. With the white grease pencil, draw the runes Raidho and Algiz (see Chapter 7) on the side of the tire that will face inside when mounted on the rim, saying, *"Be sure and solid; grip well the road; be light in your treads for quick maneuvering when required. Let it be so."*

3. Repeat with the three other tires. If you have a fourth for a full-sized spare, repeat it for that as well.
4. Have the tires placed on the car as usual.

PROTECTING YOURSELF ON PUBLIC TRANSPORT

Review the Basic Shield spell in Chapter 2 and the Invisibility Spell earlier in this chapter. Both of these are invaluable when traveling in public. The Visualization Spell for Vehicles earlier in this chapter is also excellent to perform as soon as you sit down on a bus or in a subway or train car.

Transit Pass Spell

This spell enchants your transit pass for smooth travel.

What You Need:
Transit pass

What to Do:

1. Center and ground.
2. With your finger, draw the Raidho and Eihwaz runes (see Chapter 7) for successful travel.
3. Say,

   May my journeys with you be safe and productive.
   May you never be lost, and may I never be lost while using you.
   May my movements always be smooth and trouble-free,
   Quick and direct,
   Never canceled or delayed.
   Let it be so.

TIP

- If you have a case for your transit pass, draw the Raidho and Eihwaz runes for successful travel on it as well.

PROTECTING YOURSELF IN NEW AND UNFAMILIAR PLACES

These spells cover protecting yourself in an environment you are not familiar with. This would include protection when you are in other countries or even other towns or states for the first time. It can also include areas of town you've never been in.

DOUBLE YOUR PROTECTION
If you're traveling to another country for a vacation or business, review the Passport Protection spell earlier in this chapter too.

Paper Bead Protection Charm

This spell uses homemade paper beads to create a protection charm to be tied to keys, bags, purses, belts, or luggage while you travel. Patterned paper can be very pretty for this project. Just make sure one side is blank so you can write on it.

What You Need:

Sheet of patterned paper, at least 4 inches × 6 inches
Ruler
Pen or pencil
Scissors
White glue
Bamboo skewer(s)
Mod Podge or other craft varnish or glaze
Paintbrush
Cord (black, red, or blue is ideal)

What to Do:

1. Set the paper on your workspace, blank side up. Using the ruler and pencil or pen, draw as many 1½-inch × 6-inch isosceles triangles as you wish (or as many as fit). Remember to keep the point in line with the middle of the base. Cut them out.

2. Write out a protection invocation of your own devising or use this one:

   As I go about my day, I am protected.
   As I walk, sing, work, rest, I am protected.
   My safety is ensured.

3. Put a dot of white glue near the tip of a triangle. Lay the bamboo skewer along the short base of the triangle and begin to roll the paper tightly around it. Press the tip with the glue against the rolled paper. If the glue doesn't stick, add another dot of glue.

4. Paint a light layer of Mod Podge or other craft varnish over the surface of the rolled bead and allow it to dry.

5. Repeat with as many other beads as you would like to make or have the supplies for.

6. When the beads are dry, slide them carefully off the skewer(s).

7. String each bead on a 6-inch length of cord. Tie them to purses, backpacks, and/or luggage.

TIPS

- Instead of craft varnish, you can use a solution of one part white glue to two parts water.

- For a glossier bead, add more layers of varnish, allowing the bead to dry thoroughly between applications.

- If you like, you can use white paper for this craft and color the reverse side with permanent markers to design your own beads. (Washable markers will run when the glaze is applied.)

- You can also add these beads to charm bags or protection pouches.

To Avoid Getting Lost

Getting lost in an unfamiliar place can be stressful. Use this quick and easy spell to help you return to your home base.

What to Do:

1. When you leave your hotel, Airbnb, or hostel in the morning, crouch down and put your hand on the doorstep. Trace the shape of a foot with your finger.
2. Straighten up and place your foot in the outline. Say, *"Wherever I wander, my feet will return here, safely and on time."*

TIP

- If you feel a little odd about doing this right in the doorway of where you're staying, you can use a landmark close by instead, such as a fountain or a mailbox.

Protecting Yourself While Walking

Whether walking to work or sightseeing in a foreign country, you can feel a bit exposed on foot. A new pair of footwear is an excellent opportunity to make some defensive magic that will be with you on a daily basis.

What You Need:

Piece of paper large enough to place shoes on
Shoes (new or otherwise)
Salt
Dish of Blessed Water (see Chapter 3)

What to Do:

1. Center and ground.
2. Lay out the paper. Place your footwear on the paper. Draw a circle around the shoes. (Don't worry about making it a perfect circle; it's the idea of something surrounding the shoes that's important.)

3. Carefully pour a line of salt along the line of the circle. When it is complete, say, *"As this circle encloses my shoes, keeping them safe, so, too, does this salt. Keep me safe from danger when these are on my feet."*
4. Carefully sprinkle the Blessed Water on the soles of the shoes.

TIPS

- If you used salt in the creation of your Blessed Water, be careful with the solution when anointing the soles to keep from marking the upper material of the shoes.

- For a winter boot version, say, *"Give me traction; keep my steps safe and my dignity intact. May my feet never be bogged down in slush or snowbanks. Keep my feet warm and safe from frostbite."*

PROTECTING YOURSELF IN THE WORKPLACE

The workplace, whether school or a career-based location, is a very specific setting. It's not home, but you spend a lot of time and invest a lot of energy in what you do there. The next section of spells focuses on problems or situations in the workplace that call for attention.

Workplace Safety

If you work in a physically dangerous environment, here's a daily spell you can perform to reinforce your safety while working.

What You Need:
Your safety equipment (e.g., steel-toe boots, hard hats, safety glasses, safety vest, and so on)

What to Do:

1. Center and ground.
2. On your safety equipment, draw the Algiz rune, the Eihwaz rune, and the Tiwaz rune (see Chapter 7).
3. Say, *"Protect me well; I thank you for your constant defense."*

TIPS

- Renew this weekly or each time you put your equipment on.
- Enhance this spell by keeping a brown jasper and a quartz crystal in your locker or the work bag in which you carry your equipment.

Hit Your Deadlines

One of the most stressful things involved with work is deadlines. They're a necessary evil because they help you schedule partial deliveries and keep on track with other departments. Sometimes there's wiggle room, but isn't it better not to need it? This spell can relieve some of the pressure.

What You Need:

Small clear vial or bottle
    with a screw-on cap
Light oil (e.g., almond,
    grapeseed)
Pinch of dried mint
Pinch of dried chamomile
Pinch of fine glitter
    (optional)
Quartz chip

What to Do:

1. Center and ground.
2. Fill the vial or bottle ¾ full with the oil.
3. Add the dried mint, chamomile, and glitter (if using). Add the quartz chip. Screw on the lid.

4. Place the bottle near your workstation. When you feel antsy about your deadline, take three deep breaths while holding the bottle. Swirl it gently to watch the contents move, then gently settle again. Say, *"I have this project under control."*

TIP

- If you have a small smoky quartz or a smoky quartz chip, add it to the bottle. (Reduce the liquid to make sure you have room for it.) Smoky quartz helps reduce anxiety.

This spell calls for a quartz chip. You can find strings of these at beading stores if you don't have a new age shop or a lapidary in your area. Having quartz chips on hand is great; you can add one to nearly any spell for an extra power boost.

Navigating Office Politics

Does someone have it in for you? Is someone undercutting your authority or poisoning your position? Is someone telling tales to your thesis supervisor? Who it is doesn't matter. This spell will help you sweeten the situation.

What You Need:

Small clear vial or bottle
  with a screw-on cap
Distilled water

Light corn syrup
9 cloves
Small smoky quartz

What to Do:

1. Center and ground.
2. Pour the water and the corn syrup into the jar, saying, *"Syrup sweetens the atmosphere around me."*
3. Drop the cloves into the liquid, saying, *"Nine cloves to stop gossip."*

4. Add the smoky quartz, saying, *"Smoky quartz to defend against hostility."*
5. Screw on the lid and shake to combine. Say, *"This spell defends me against those who would oppose me. Let communication regarding me be sweet and positive. It is so."*
6. Keep the bottle in a drawer at work or in your locker.

TIPS

• Review the sections on protecting yourself emotionally and mentally in Chapter 2 to help support this spell.

The proportions for the liquid in this bottle are 1 part corn syrup to 2 parts water. Use your chosen container to measure it out. Remember to leave room for the additional components to be added. The total volume of liquid should only take up ⅔ of the entire bottle to be safe.

Dealing with Sexual Harassment

There's been a lot of news about sexual harassment lately and for good reason. People have been getting away with it for far too long. Speaking up can be terrifying, but for the love of everything good, talk to your HR department. Here's a spell to defend yourself against harassment and gaslighting and to give yourself a boost to have the courage to speak out about it.

What You Need:

Dragon's blood incense and censer
Matches or lighter
3 cloves
1 tablespoon stinging nettle

Black pouch or bag
Amethyst
Tiger's eye
Black tourmaline
Rose quartz

What to Do:

1. Ground and center.
2. Light the dragon's blood incense. Say, *"I am a valuable person. My voice deserves to be heard."*
3. Place the cloves and the stinging nettle into the black pouch.
4. Place the amethyst into the pouch, saying, *"The truth is brought to light."*
5. Place the tiger's eye into the pouch, saying, *"My body is defended; this crisis is resolved."*
6. Place the black tourmaline into the pouch, saying, *"I will outlast this."*
7. Place the rose quartz into the pouch, saying, *"I am worthy of love and respect. All negativity directed at me is transformed to light."*
8. Close the pouch. Pass it through the incense smoke three times, then leave it next to the censer until the incense burns down.
9. Carry the pouch with you at work.

Protect Your Job and Career

It's a tough world out there, with jobs being phased out and companies downsizing. Employment is precious, especially if yours is the sole income in the family. Good objects to use in this spell include a pay stub, an employment contract, an NDA—anything legal pertaining to your job.

What You Need:

Contract or legal documents pertaining to your employment
Green candle and holder
Gold candle and holder
Matches or lighter
Blue pouch or bag
Pinch of basil
Section of cinnamon stick
Pinch of nutmeg
Pinch of peppermint
Tiger's eye

What to Do:

1. Center and ground.
2. Place the document(s) in the center of your workspace.
3. Place the green and gold candles on either side and light them, saying, *"Success and long employment are mine."*
4. Place the basil in the pouch, followed by the cinnamon stick, nutmeg, and peppermint.
5. Place the tiger's eye in the pouch and close it. Lay it on the documents between the candles and repeat, *"Success and long employment are mine. I continue to be employed in the field of my choosing, in a position that values me and uses my skills with suitable remuneration. It is so."*

TIP

• This spell specifically does *not* call to make your current job or career permanent forever. That could cause problems when you decide it's time to move on to a better position somewhere else or opt for a career change.

Protect Your Supplies

Do your tools go AWOL? Does someone always walk off with your pens? Have you had to request a new stapler from the supply department so many times that they think you're running a stapler store on the side? Make sure your supplies come back to you.

What You Need:
Your office supplies and/or tools

What to Do:

1. Center and ground.
2. With your finger, draw a spiral on your desk. The spiral should start from the outside and spiral inward. At the center of the spiral, without lifting your finger, draw a straight line down, crossing the bottom half of the spiral, and draw an arrowhead on the end of that line.
3. Draw the same symbol on the bottom of each of your tools or supplies, saying, *"Return, return, return"* as you do.

Protect Against Equipment Failure

Equipment failure is dreaded with good reason. Back up in multiple places! Carry a USB drive. Email your current work to yourself at the end of the day. And use this spell regularly to reduce the chances of your equipment losing your thesis, a critical presentation, or your entire digital portfolio. Brown jasper is good for long-term protection, and obsidian is good at drawing out toxins. Together, these two stones can help protect your equipment from conking out. The Thurisaz rune is associated with using tools in your work.

What You Need:
Brown jasper
Obsidian

What to Do:

1. Cleanse the stones according to your chosen method from Chapter 7.
2. Hold the stones in your hands. Close your eyes and visualize a light radiating out from the stones, stretching out to encompass your equipment.

3. Say,

Creatures of earth, creatures of rock,
Lend your energy to my will.
Defend this machine,
Keep it strong,
May it stay true until I no longer need it.

4. With your finger, draw the Thurisaz rune on each stone (see Chapter 7). Draw the Thurisaz rune on your piece of equipment as well.

5. Place the stones on top of the equipment. If this isn't possible, you can slip them into a tiny bag and hang it nearby or use a puttylike adhesive to stick them on the side of the machine. If none of this is possible, put them in a drawer nearby.

PART 3:
RITUALS AND PROTECTIVE OBJECTS

CHAPTER 6:
RITUALS

Sometimes you need more than a spell. These rituals are longer and more detailed, and they involve more energy and more focus. They accordingly provide a more complex level of protection. These rituals are excellent foundations upon which to add levels of defense with spells.

HOUSE PROTECTION RITUAL

This ritual sets up a relatively permanent shield around your home. It begins by cleansing, banishing any negativity from the site so as to have a clean slate from which to construct the new defenses. It then sets up protection by blessing with all the elements and anchoring energy wards around the site.

An advance warning: your energy is used to direct the construction of this shield. You will be responsible for maintaining it, or it will gradually fade.

This is a two-part ritual and has been divided for ease of performance. Do the second half right after the first half, though.

House Protection Ritual Part 1: Banishing

Prior to a more elaborate ritual such as this, a cleansing or removal of non-supportive energy is done. It may seem like an extra step that just takes up more time, but it provides a good, solid foundation for what will follow. Banishing is traditionally done in a counterclockwise motion, to push away.

What You Need:

Broom
Tray
Candle and candleholder
Matches or lighter

Incense and censer
Bowl or cup of water
Small dish of salt

What to Do:

1. Tidy the house. Put things away, straighten up, wash handprints and splashes off the walls, wipe down counters, vacuum, and so forth. Physical dirt and clutter should be removed in order to offer the best possible base for this ritual to be as successful as possible.

2. Center and ground.

3. Say, *"I banish from the space any negative energy."*

4. For each step, start at the front door and move counterclockwise through the house. Move counterclockwise through each room as you come to it.

5. With the broom, start sweeping the floor with a counterclockwise motion, visualizing the broom disturbing any negative energy. Break it up with the broom. Move through each room of the house and finish at the front door.

6. On the tray, place the candle in the holder, matches or lighter, incense and censer, bowl or cup of water, and small dish of salt. Light the candle and the incense. Put three pinches of salt into the water and swirl it gently to combine.

7. Carry the tray to the first room and place it in the center on the floor or on a nearby level surface. Pick up the incense and carry it counterclockwise around the room, waving the smoke into the corners, saying, *"I cleanse you with air."* Return the censer to the tray. Pick up the candle and carry it counterclockwise through the room, saying, *"I cleanse you with the light of fire,"* then replace it on the tray. Carry the dish of salt water counterclockwise around the room, dipping your fingers into it and sprinkling drops around, saying, *"I cleanse you with water and earth."*

8. Continue counterclockwise through the house, cleansing each room. Finish by doing the area by the front door.

House Protection Ritual Part 2: Protecting

Once your space is clear of any energy that might work contrary to your purpose, it's time to protect it. Drawing something toward you is traditionally done in a clockwise motion.

What You Need:

Small dish of olive oil

Pinch of rosemary

Pinch of salt

Tray from Part 1

Candle and candleholder
from Part 1

Incense and censer
from Part 1

Bowl or cup of salt water
from Part 1

What to Do:

1. Center and ground.
2. Say, *"I call protective energy to bless this space."*
3. Place rosemary and salt into the olive oil; swirl gently to combine.
4. Moving clockwise through the house, take the tray into each room. Carry the incense clockwise around the room, saying, *"I bless you with air."* Carry the candle around the room, saying, *"I bless you with fire."* Carry the salt water around the room, saying, *"I bless you with water and earth."*
5. When the room has been blessed, take the bowl of oil and dip your finger in it. Draw the Algiz rune (see Chapter 7) on the window or window frame.
6. Continue through the house in a clockwise direction, repeating all the steps in each room. Draw the Algiz rune on each door to the exterior as well as every window. Finish at the front door again.
7. Center and ground again at the front door, draw up energy from the ground, and let it flow through your arms down to your hands. Walk clockwise through the house again, drawing a barrier with that energy. You don't have to go into each room; pause in the doorway and project the energy. The goal is to line the outside walls with the energy barrier. Energy passes through walls, so don't worry about the interior walls; just project along the exterior.

8. Complete the clockwise circuit through the house and join the energy with the first part of the barrier so it forms a complete circle (or oval, rectangle, or whatever shape your house is).

9. Visualize the energy barrier arching up over the house and curving down underneath it until the edges meet above and below, encasing the house in a sphere or egg shape.

10. Before you release it entirely, visualize a tendril or conduit extending down from the barrier by your front door deep into the earth until it meets with the energy of the earth, just as you do when grounding. Visualize the tendril rooting itself in that energy so it is always connected to an energy source.

HOUSE PROTECTION MAINTENANCE

This major house protection should be checked on a regular basis for weak spots. Review the suggested maintenance protocols in Chapter 3. Walk through the house with your senses extended, feeling for places that might need a bit of extra energy applied to them.

As suggested in the maintenance protocols in Chapter 3, scheduling a regular inspection is constructive. It helps you keep a finger on the pulse of the energy and how it's behaving in your home, so to speak.

Remember to take this shield up before you move. If you don't, it will fade over time with no one maintaining it, even though it is tied into the earth's energy. However, this is more a matter of courtesy. It is uncomfortable for the next owner or tenant to walk in and feel like they're being watched or feel uncomfortable for some reason in a space that was previously magically maintained by someone else.

PROTECTING AN OBJECT

Sometimes, you want to specifically protect a single object instead of using a general protection spell for a room or a house. Maybe you're lending it to someone, or will be taking it out of the house and are worried about its energy being affected. Perhaps you're bringing something new into your home, and want it to be purified and protected before you introduce it to the rest of your home's energy. Whatever the reason, this ritual offers you a way to cleanse and protect an object.

Full Ritual for Protecting an Object

This ritual for protecting an object uses the energy-absorbing properties of salt to remove any unwanted energy from an item before anointing it with an herbal wash made from water and protective herbs. It's easy to do, and while it seems basic, the impact it has on the energy of the object is significant. You can use either plain iodized table salt or coarse or fine sea salt for this ritual.

What You Need:

Item to be purified and protected	Salt
	Small glass
Clean cloth	Water
Bowl or plate large enough to hold the item	Sprig of fresh rosemary
	Sprig of fresh basil

What to Do:

1. Wipe down the object with the clean cloth.
2. Fill the bowl or plate with salt. It doesn't have to be deep; just cover the bottom of the dish so the item touches the salt with as much of its surface as possible.
3. Place the item on the salt. Don't bury it. Say, *"[Item], by this salt you will be cleansed. By this salt, you are purified. By this salt, all negative energy clinging to you is removed."*
4. Place the dish in a spot where it won't be disturbed. A sunny spot is ideal as the sunlight will boost the banishing of the negative energy, but it isn't necessary.

5. Leave the item for 3 days.

6. On the third day, pour fresh water into the glass. Into it place the sprigs of fresh rosemary and basil. Allow them to steep for at least 3 hours.

7. Remove the item from the bed of salt. Wipe it down again with the clean cloth.

8. Remove the sprigs of rosemary and basil from the herbal water. Gently stroke the wet sprigs over the item, dipping them into the water again as needed, saying, *"[Item], by these herbs you are protected. By these herbs, you are defended. By these herbs, you are safe."*

9. Dispose of the salt by flushing it down the toilet or washing it gradually down the drain while running the cold water from the faucet. Pour the herbal water outdoors. Compost the herbal sprigs or dispose of them outdoors with the water.

TIPS

- For extra power, time this spell to take place the day before, the day of, and the day after a full moon.

- Many grocery stores have packages of fresh herbs in the produce department. But if you can't get fresh sprigs of rosemary and basil, put a pinch of each of the dried versions into the water instead. Use your fingers to anoint the object with the water.

PROTECTING A PERSON

Remember, doing magic for or on someone who has not given you permission means that you consent to accepting all the consequences of doing it. There are times when you will gladly accept this karmic burden—for example, if a friend is missing. However, it is best to obtain his or her permission.

This ritual uses the concept of sympathetic magic to protect an individual. Sympathetic magic posits that whatever happens to a representation of something will also happen to the thing it represents. For this ritual, since you are protecting a person, you will need a representation of that individual.

What kind of representation is up to you. You can use a photograph, draw a picture, sew a simple person-shaped poppet (see Chapter 2), or even use a LEGO mini-figure or another toy. If you're creating the image, do your best to make it look like the person you're doing the ritual for. The closer the resemblance, the more effective the spell. If the person always wears a specific necklace, add one to your representation; reproduce an iconic hairstyle or favorite T-shirt, add a birthmark…you get the idea.

Full Ritual for Protecting a Person

This version of the ritual uses a LEGO mini-figure. Before you start the ritual, personalize the mini-figure as best you can. Add details with paint, plasticine, or other modeling compound if you like.

What You Need:
6 amethysts

Cedar incense and censer

Matches or lighter

White silk square or cotton
    handkerchief

1 tablespoon angelica

1 tablespoon stinging nettle

Blue pouch or bag

What to Do:

1. Cleanse the stones and the figure according to your preferred method in Chapter 7.
2. Center and ground.
3. Cast a circle (see Chapter 1).
4. Light the cedar incense.
5. Spread the white silk out on your workspace.

6. Hold the figure and say, *"You are [name of person to be protected]."*
7. Lay the figure down in the center of the white silk square. Place the six amethysts around it in an oval, saying, *"Your body is protected."*
8. Sprinkle the angelica around the figure, saying, *"Your heart is protected."*
9. Sprinkle the stinging nettle around the figure, saying, *"Your mind is protected."*
10. Carefully fold in the edges and corners of the silk, wrapping the figure, stones, and herbs. Pass the packet through the incense smoke, saying, *"Thus are you defended against attack and misfortune; thus are you protected against evil and pain. It is so."*
11. Carefully place the wrapped figure into the blue pouch and close it. Leave the pouch by the censer until the incense has burned down.
12. Keep the pouch in a safe place.
13. Later, when the time comes, light another stick of cedar incense and respectfully open the pouch. Remove the figure, set it on your workspace, and unwrap it carefully, saying, *"The period of supportive magic has served its time. Thank you for allowing me to help protect you. Call on me should you again need help."* Remove the personalization you did on the mini-figure and wash it in salt water to help cleanse it. Cleanse the stones as well and compost the herbs.

TIP

• This is not a permanent spell. It will fade over time. More importantly, it *shouldn't* be a permanent spell. While this spell can provide magical protection for a time, it's important to allow people to work out their own solutions.

CHAPTER 7:
PROTECTIVE OBJECTS

Everything has an energy to it. This section provides lists and reference information regarding herbs, stones, symbols, and other things that offer magical energy to support your protection spellwork. These lists are by no means exhaustive. They are selections of common and particularly useful examples in relation to protection. It's worth researching and reading further to absorb more information like this, to help fine-tune your protection magic. For example, working a spell to protect your finances? Look up herbs and stones specifically associated with money or prosperity to involve with the stones and herbs you're already using that resonate with protective energy.

After working through some of the spells in this book, you may feel like putting together a spell of your own. The information in this chapter can help you with that. For more information and an in-depth look at crafting your own spells, please see my book *Power Spellcraft for Life*.

COLORS ASSOCIATED WITH PROTECTION

One of the easiest ways to add protective energy to your life is to use color. An important fact before you begin: everyone responds to color differently. It's important to explore your relationship with a color before using it in spellwork. For example, if you have horrible child-hood associations with the color red, as my mother does, using red in spellwork designed to make you feel safe and centered is a terrible idea. Take time to think through colors and record your emotional responses to them. You may find that yellow resonates with protective energy the most strongly for you, for example.

THINK ABOUT YOUR CONNECTIONS

Always consider your personal connections to a list of supplies. Following an existing spell when you disagree with the supplies or have established that some of them don't work well for you is a recipe for failure. There's no point putting in the energy and time. Either research a substitute or look for another spell.

That said, here's a short list of colors commonly associated with protection or defense:

- Black: Dispels negative energy, absorbs negativity, repels evil
- White: Purifies, soothes, represents wholeness and new beginnings
- Blue: Cleanses, purifies negativity, encourages truth and communication
- Red: Power, energy, stopping or removing something
- Gold: Energy, success, health

Other colors that can support your spellwork in some of the areas covered in this book include:

- Yellow: Happiness and joy, clarity, communication, safe travels, happy home
- Green: Healing, calm, property/possessions, finances
- Brown: Transformation, earth, property
- Orange: Abundance, career, acceptance, self-esteem, motivation

HOW TO INCORPORATE COLOR INTO YOUR SPELLWORK

Apart from using candles in the colors just mentioned, how can you pull more color-related energy into your spellwork? There are lots of ways! Here are some suggestions:

- Write out spells or written elements in colored pencil, pens, or markers.
- Spread a colored cloth over your workspace.
- Wear clothing or jewelry in a color associated with the spellwork you're doing.
- If a spell calls for thread or cord, use colored.
- If a spell calls for a jar or bottle, use a colored one.

CRYSTALS, STONES, AND GEMS FOR PROTECTION

Many of the stones in this section are called for in the spells collected in this book. Here's a handy reference to the stones most often used in protection magic as well as information on how to prepare them and ways to use them.

You can work with a basic collection of stones. You often don't need to throw away or otherwise write off the stones you use in spells unless they're designated to become part of an ongoing process or carried as part of a charm or talisman bag. A lot of the time, they're used to enhance the effects of an empowering or charging process, but after that they can be reused. Cleanse the stones according to one of the processes in this chapter and put them back in your box or bag of stones to be used in future spells.

Here's a handy reference for the stones most often used in protection magic:

AMETHYST

Amethyst is a form of purple quartz. It's excellent for protection of body and mind, success, defense, and bringing the truth to light. It is said to guard against drunkenness as well as overexcitement, allowing you to keep a clear head. It can defend against unexpected attack, betrayal, and weather.

BLACK TOURMALINE

Excellent for protection from destructive energy and for increasing self-confidence and endurance in difficult situations. It can help you discover a guilty party or the source of trouble and protect you against people who endlessly draw on your energy. Black tourmaline doesn't just reflect or deflect negative energy; it can transform it into positive energy for you to use. It can be used for grounding, purification, and relief from stress.

CLEAR QUARTZ

An extremely versatile stone, clear quartz is one of the ultimate stones to use in protection magic. It excels at protecting body, mind, heart, and spirit from negativity. This multipurpose stone is popular in new age practice because it can function like a battery, providing an alternate energy source. Quartz cheerfully allows you to use its energy, and there's plenty of it to borrow. Clear quartz is good for enhancing any sort of spell. If you charge it to absorb negativity, it can do that too; quartz is very receptive to programming or charging with a specific intention.

HEMATITE

A dull silver-toned stone, hematite looks a bit like a clouded mirror. And like a mirror, it's good at reflecting energy. Hematite can be used to deflect negative energy away from you. Hematite is also used to help ground energy, so if you're dazed or feeling nervous, reach for hematite. It strengthens courage, confidence, optimism, and focus.

MALACHITE

Malachite is associated with the natural environment. It's excellent for use in a situation in which unwanted influence is coming from your environment because it can transmute that energy into beneficial energy. It can filter pollution, noise, and other harmful environmental effects. It is also used to protect health and encourage healing as well as promoting balance. It is particularly good for protection in jobs associated with working with the earth or travel.

OBSIDIAN

Black obsidian is good to use after shock or trauma to protect fragile energy and defend against any further negativity during the healing process. It is an essential stone in protecting against negative energy. It can protect you against sadness, bullying, and illusions (including gaslighting and negging) and help ground negativity. In this way, it can also support self-confidence and self-esteem.

Snowflake obsidian is particularly helpful in working to protect yourself against your own destructive thinking and encouraging transformation. It's a centering and grounding stone, good to use as protection against mental, emotional, and physical attacks. It helps release negativity from people and spaces and helps unblock energy as well.

JASPER

Jasper comes in many colors, and most of them strengthen courage and protect against danger. It is often used as a worry stone to help keep you balanced and even tempered. Red jasper specifically emphasizes justice, stamina, stability, endurance, and guarding against physical threat. Brown jasper is particularly good at guarding your energy over a long period of time and keeping you safe in long-term stressful situations.

ROSE QUARTZ

The ultimate stone to enhance good vibrations! Rose quartz is a lovely stone that attracts and amplifies positive energy while dispelling negativity. It's used for love, self-esteem, self-trust, and comfort. Using rose quartz in a multiperson situation will help create better bonds among all involved. It's a wonderful stone to use for children and friends as well as in healing situations in which emotional or mental trauma has also been experienced. It can also guard against malicious gossip.

SMOKY QUARTZ

Excellent for absorbing negative energy and for protection against negative thinking, smoky quartz relieves stress and panic attacks, which is helpful when facing an unknown or dangerous situation. It is excellent to use for grounding and helping you to regain focus and concentration. Like other quartzes, smoky quartz can absorb negative energy. It can be used to guard the home or car against theft and protect a driver from problems on the road. It's good for protection against hostility in the workplace and as a defense against bullying.

TIGER'S EYE

Tiger's eye is a stone associated with stability, strength, and grounding. It offers protection against physical harm and bad luck while encouraging you to be strong and confident. It is good to use as protection against the negative thoughts of others.

PREPARING AND CLEANSING STONES

Stones are useful elements in spellwork because they can be recycled by cleansing and purifying them. This removes any previous energy coded into them as well as any stray energy they have collected along the way. (Don't worry; it doesn't remove their native energy.) Once a stone has been cleansed, it's ready to be used as a blank slate again.

There are several ways to cleanse a stone.

SALT

A good way to cleanse a stone is to bury it in a small dish of salt for at least a day, longer if you feel the stone has heavy programming or has collected a lot of junky energy.

CHECK THE METAL CONTENT

Warning: stones with a high iron content react poorly to salt, so check first. Likewise, if the stone is in any kind of metal setting, choose another cleansing method; the salt will damage the metal of the setting.

Use any kind of salt you have on hand. You might want to keep the more expensive salt for actual spellwork, though.

EARTH

Bury the stone in a small dish of earth for three or more days. Earth from your garden is fine, as is earth from a bag of potting soil. You can use a potted houseplant for this, marking the spot with a toothpick so you can locate the stone when it's time. However, choose another method if the stone contains a lot of negative energy; that energy will be absorbed by the earth (which is the point of using the earth to cleanse the stone), but it will in turn be absorbed from the earth into the houseplant.

WATER

Pour bottled spring water in a dish and set the stone in it. Water is an excellent purifier. If you add a pinch of salt to it, it becomes even more powerful. However, if there's any metal attached to or within the stone, skip the salt and use pure water.

SUNLIGHT AND MOONLIGHT

The easiest of the cleansing techniques involves setting your stone on a windowsill where the direct sunlight or moonlight will hit it. Judge how long to leave it according to how much cleansing you feel the stone needs. You can set the stone on a mirror to enhance the effect.

GODS, SAINTS, AND ANGELS

As spellwork isn't bound to a religion, anyone of any path can use it. That said, there is a long tradition of invoking spiritual figures in spellwork. It hasn't been done in this book because these spells are designed to be used by anyone of any religious path. If you feel like calling on gods, saints, or angels to help in your spellwork, go right ahead. Sometimes it can be as easy as adding a sentence like *"In the name of [religious figure], let it be so."*

The list of figures here isn't exhaustive by any means; it suggests the kinds of figures you can look for to support your protective spellcraft. However, it isn't ideal to start invoking entities you aren't familiar with. It's best to learn more about a figure before you call on it, so do some reading and research before blithely invoking a deity.

CHRISTIAN FIGURES

Here are some figures from Christianity to call on for help in protection magic:

- Archangel Michael: Associated with the South and the element of fire, Michael is usually portrayed in armor holding a sword or scepter. He is a warrior, associated with justice, loyalty, and defense.
- Saint Christopher: Associated with good luck and travel.
- Saint Rita: Associated with lonely people, Rita is the patron saint of abused women, bad marriages, and widows.

GODS AND GODDESSES

Many deities were appealed to for help in their particular fields. Here is a brief list of deities from different cultures who were specifically associated with defense and protection:

- Athena: (Greek) Defensive war, wisdom, strategy
- Bellona: (Roman) Defense, war, success
- Tyr: (Norse) Success, war, order, law
- Lakshmi: (Hindu) Good fortune, recovering from hardship

- Vishnu: (Hindu) Protection, preservation, order
- Isis: (Egyptian) Protector of women and children, healing
- Horus: (Egyptian) Protection, healing
- Green Tara: (Buddhist) Peace, protection, deflecting negative energy

In researching deities to work with in protection spellwork, look for those associated with war, peace, good fortune, good health or healing, and harmony. If your protection spellwork focuses on a specific issue, research deities associated with that subject. For example, if you are doing spellwork to protect your finances, look for deities associated with money to call upon.

ANIMALS

Calling on the energy or power of strong animals is a practice found in a variety of cultures. Here are some animals associated with defense and protection that you can call on for support in your spellwork.

THINK ABOUT YOUR PREFERENCES TOO
If you already have an affinity for a particular animal, call on that animal for help, even if it isn't necessarily explicitly associated with protection. You have a connection with that animal, and that can be enough.

- Lion: Courage, patience, power, strength; a guardian figure in several cultures
- Dragon: Strength, courage, power, luck, fortune, change
- Eagle: Challenges, courage, resilience, clarity, wisdom
- Wolf: Pack, caring for others, teacher, freedom, intuition

HERBS FOR PROTECTION

Herbs are a wonderfully accessible way to work with natural energies to enhance your protection. They're discreet, versatile, and fun to play with.

Herbs like bay, sage, rosemary, cloves, and cinnamon are likely already in your spice rack, along with salt. Nettle, cedar, and juniper can be collected from outdoors. Angelica and rue may be harder to find, but both can be grown. Other plants may have to be purchased from an herb shop or ordered online.

In general, unless otherwise specified, herbs are used dried. If you have sprigs of a fresh herb and a spell calls for it to be used in a pouch or some other way that should be dry, you can spread the herb sprigs in a single layer on a parchment-lined baking sheet and place them in an oven at low heat (no more than 175°F) for anywhere between 90 minutes to 4 hours, depending on their moisture content. Keep the oven door cracked open and after an hour, check on the herbs every 15 minutes or so. When you can crumble the leaves between your fingers, remove the sheet from the oven and allow the herbs to cool. Light or fine sprigs of herbs will dry faster than thicker herbs.

Once they're dry, you can either store the sprigs whole in a tightly closed jar or crumble the leaves off the stems and put them in spice jars.

SEPARATE HERBS?

Do you have to keep your magical herbs separate from your cooking herbs? That's up to you. Some people do, and some don't. If you're comfortable grabbing a spoonful of rosemary from the spice jar in the pantry, go for it. You'll be purifying it anyway. If you're not comfortable, that's fine too. Keep a second set of herbs with your spellworking supplies.

Here's a list of basic protective herbs:

ANGELICA (*ANGELICA ARCHANGELICA*)

Angelica has powerful protective energy. It can be used to ward off disease and illness, bad luck, and evil and to protect a home. It also reinforces personal courage, particularly when you occupy a morally upright position. Angelica can be carried alone as a powerful protective amulet. Grown in a garden, it extends its protective energy to the house and property.

BAY LEAVES (*LAURUS NOBILIS*)

The leaves of the bay laurel are excellent for protection, to enhance wisdom, to remove negativity, for good luck, and for money. Bay also is used to guard health and to celebrate victory.

CEDAR (*CEDRUS* SPP.)

Cedar is a strong purifier, clearing negative energy and leaving a very positive energy in its place. It can help protect from unwanted influences, repel evil, encourage positivity and benevolence, and support healing. You can use the ground wood, dried and chopped cedar fronds, or shredded bark.

CINNAMON (*CINNAMOMUM VERUM, CINNAMOMUM CASSIA*)

Cinnamon is good for protection, activity, energy, money, healing, and love. You can add a pinch of cinnamon to a spell that needs a strong injection of energy and action.

CLOVE (*SYZYGIUM AROMATICUM*)

Cloves are excellent for stopping rumors, killing gossip, and protecting your reputation from unjust accusations. They invite good luck, promote prosperity and positive financial dealings, and have healing energy.

GARLIC (*ALLIUM SATIVUM*)

Garlic is used to strengthen resolution, to enhance bravery, for defense against evil, and to improve and protect health. It can be carried to defend against the theft of your energy, intentional or otherwise. Braids of garlic hung in the house can absorb negativity and misfortune. Garlic can be used fresh or dried.

JUNIPER (*JUNIPERUS COMMUNIS*)

Juniper has a strong protective energy. It is particularly good at protecting against theft of any kind and against accidents. Juniper is used to attract good luck, to support health, to reduce anxiety, to improve focus and clarity, and for purification. Juniper can be used in the form of ground or shaved wood, shredded bark, or berries.

LEMON (*CITRUS LIMON*)

Purifying and clarifying, lemon can also be added to spells for joy and clear communication. It is good for dispelling murky or sluggish energy and deflecting negativity. Depending on the spell, you can use fresh lemons, lemon juice, or dried lemon zest.

NETTLE (*URTICA DIOICA*)

Stinging nettles are excellent to use in defensive magic, especially spells that reverse energy and send it back to its source. They are also used for healing, courage, and avoiding danger. Fresh nettles should be handled with gloves. The herb is usually used dried and chopped.

ONION (*ALLIUM CEPA*)

Onions are used for protection and exorcism as well as banishing illness and negative influences. The onion's ability to absorb negative energy makes it a common element of defensive magic.

ROSEMARY (*ROSMARINUS OFFICINALIS*)

Rosemary is good for protection, removing negative energy, and enhancing memory. Use rosemary for positive thinking as well, a bonus in any kind of spellwork! This herb enhances confidence and dispels negativity.

RUE (*RUTA GRAVEOLENS*)

Also called herb of grace, rue has a long history of being associated with protection, banishing, and warding. Sprigs of it can be used to sprinkle Blessed Water or infusions over people or places, a practice known as asperging. Sprigs of rue used to be hung over doors and windows to keep away illness, misfortune, and negative energy.

SAGE (*SALVIA* SPP.*)

Sage is excellent for purification of any kind. The traditional smudge stick is made from sage or a base of sage with other cleansing herbs. Growing sage is said to lengthen the lifespan, making it an excellent herb to use in spellwork involving healing or strengthening health. Sage can be a very calming herb and is also associated with prosperity, wisdom, and business. In fact, the Roman word *salvia* means "to protect, save, or heal."

Any kind of sage can be used. The most common type is culinary sage, *Salvia officianalis*, easily found in supermarkets in the spice section. In esoteric shops you may also find white sage (*Salvia apiana*), blue sage (*Salvia clevelandii*), purple or lavender sage (*Salvia leucophylla*), or black sage (*Salvia mellifera*). Not all herbs called sage are actually sage, however; double-check the Latin name to make sure.

SALT

Salt is the go-to ingredient for protection. It's technically a mineral, but salt is often classified with herbs because it's a consumable, easy to find, and easy to use.

Salt absorbs and binds energy, specifically negative energy. Sprinkling it into a bath can help draw away negative energy clinging to the physical body. It can be used to draw impure energy from objects by laying the object in a bowl or plate of salt. A simple bowl of salt placed in a room can absorb unwanted energy. Once used for cleansing or purification, salt shouldn't be reused; you can dispose of it by pouring it gradually down the sink with the water running.

Traditionally, black salt was made by mixing regular salt with iron, and this kind of black salt can still be purchased. To make it, you can use iron filed from a cast iron pot or pan or mix ash from a fire into it. Hawaiian black salt is a blend of sea salt from Hawaii and powdered coconut-shell charcoal. It's classified as food-grade salt, so it's not dangerous to use. You may also use pink Himalayan salt, although regular salt works just as well.

HOW TO PREPARE AND USE HERBS

Herbs should be cleansed before use, just as stones are. However, it's not to the same degree, as stones function differently in collecting energy. Herbs can be purified before use with this simple process:

1. Center and ground.
2. Hold your hands over the herb.
3. Draw energy up from the earth. Let it flow down your arms to your hands and to the herb.
4. Say, *"With this energy you are purified, cleared of anything not your own."*
5. The herb is ready to be used.

You can store the herb after purifying it, but it's worth sensing the energy before you use it later to see if it needs to be purified again. Purify if you're in doubt; it's quick and won't hurt.

Throughout this book, herbs have been used in spells to add their energy, either scattered around a focus during the spell itself or added to a charm bag. There are other ways to use them, however.

INFUSIONS AND DECOCTIONS

Whenever you make tea, you're making an infusion. To infuse is to steep an herb in water hot enough to extract its properties in a short amount of time. If you boil an herb in water, you make a decoction. Either method produces a liquid that, after straining, can be used for a variety of purposes, such as wiping down objects, walls, or floors; anointing the body or hair; or using in a spray bottle. An infusion or decoction can be stored in a closed jar or bottle in the fridge for a couple of days.

INFUSED HERBAL OILS

Oils are made by infusing an herb in an oil such as olive or sunflower. The easiest way to make herb-infused oil is to fill a clean jar with chopped dry herbs and slowly pour in enough oil to cover them. Stir the herbal matter to make sure the oil reaches all of it, then screw the lid on the jar and shake it gently. Leave the jar in a cool place and shake it every few days. After 3 weeks, start checking to see if the oil has infused enough. Leave it for up to 6 weeks for denser, thicker herbs; they will need the extra time for the oil to extract the herbal essence. Strain the oil through cheesecloth or another filter into clean storage bottles, squeezing the oil-soaked herbs to extract as much as possible. Label and cap the storage bottles. Use within a year. These oils can be used to draw protective symbols on windows, walls, doors, or objects; used to anoint the body; or added to a bath. (Be careful with cinnamon, which can irritate.)

INCENSE

The most easily available incense is in stick or cone form and is made of powdered wood pressed into shape (around a thin wooden center, in the case of a stick). The sticks and cones are then soaked in a blend of oils to infuse them with scent.

You can make your own incense with herbs and resins and burn it on charcoal tablets, easily found at new age shops, ethnic grocery shops, and ecclesiastical supply shops. You can burn dried herbs directly on the charcoal, but they tend to have a very strong smell and crisp very quickly. Blending dried herbal matter with a granulated resin like frankincense makes it smell sweeter, adds to the protective or purifying energies, and makes it burn a little longer. Frankincense granules can be found at new age and ecclesiastical shops or ordered online. You can add a couple of drops of essential oil to your incense blend too. Write your blend down so you can tweak or repeat the recipe in the future and clearly label the jar in which you keep the incense if you make enough to store.

SPRINKLING POWDERS

Powders are made by finely grinding dry herbs, either by hand in a mortar and pestle or in a coffee grinder devoted solely to grinding herbs. (Otherwise, you'll get coffee powder in your herbs and herbs in your coffee!) You can use them as a single ingredient, or you can combine herbs before or after powdering them.

Sprinkling powders can be used to help purify spaces. Sprinkle them on the floor, let them rest there for a bit to affect the space with their energy, then sweep them up and toss them outside. You can use pinches of herb powder in spells that call for dried herbs, sprinkle them on the doorstep, or use them to protect your property outside. Blend a pinch (or more) of herb powder into some fine rice flour or cornstarch to use as a body powder, to dust sheets on a bed, or to use as a carpet refresher.

POTPOURRI

Potpourri is a simple blend of dried herbs in a bowl or jar, sometimes enhanced with a drop or two of essential oil. The herbs may be chosen for their magical energies or for their pleasant scents. For example, you may choose to blend a pleasant-smelling combination of dried rose petals, sandalwood chips, and dried carnation petals, then add a pinch of cinnamon, some rosemary, and a few bay leaves for their protective properties.

PROTECTIVE SYMBOLS

Symbols are a type of shorthand, a design that encodes specific energies or associations, creating layers of meaning. Just as a written word conveys meaning, so, too, does a symbol. Symbols serve to identify as well as empower.

In magic, symbols are used to bless, banish, protect, and either attract or repel specific energies. Below are a handful of symbols from different cultures, all associated with defense and protection in some way.

RUNES

Runes are Germanic symbols. Part alphabet, part mystery, and part poem, the runes are more than letters. Apart from the linguistic value of each rune, they are also used as magical symbols and divination. The meaning of the term *rune* is "something secret or hidden," which underlines the esoteric connection. Each rune embodies a different spiritual secret embedded in a brief poem, which the individual must study and meditate on to achieve insight into the rune's essence. Fortunately, there is a shorthand available, a set of meanings collected over centuries that have been ascribed to each rune.

There are different related runic alphabets from different places and dating from different eras, but they have remarkable similarities. The earliest and possibly most frequently used today is the Elder Futhark, used between C.E. 150 and 800.

Here are six runes from the Elder Futhark that can be used in protection spellwork.

ALGIZ

Among other things, Algiz (sometimes called Elhaz) is one of the Elder Futhark runes associated with protection. The shape is said to represent the yew tree, a tree associated with eternity, knowledge, and protection from evil. Algiz also represents the strength of the universe; divine blessing; and protection for yourself, family, and friends. In other words, it's a terrific all-purpose rune to use for protection. It can also be used to defend your health, maintain your welfare, and strengthen your resistance to stress and attack.

THURISAZ

A rune representing strength, Thurisaz is excellent for spells focused on strength, disputes, force, defense, and breaking through obstacles. It's good to use when working against opposing forces and applying your will as a warrior in defense of you and yours.

EIHWAZ

Eihwaz is a rune of stability and strength and can be used in spell-work focusing on endurance and a continued flow of energy. It is strongly associated with personal protection and protection of personal rights. Use it on long journeys and to make sure information flows as it should. It is also associated with hunting and survival.

RAIDHO

Raidho is the rune associated with travel and motion. It encompasses being in control of your journey, common sense, confidence, and taking action instead of being passive, making it an excellent rune to use in conjunction with travel-related spellwork.

TIWAZ

Tiwaz is the rune of justice, fighting for what is right, and peacekeeping. It seeks to balance chaos with order. It is excellent to use in spellwork associated with legal matters, justice, and activism. Use this rune to protect yourself from negative influences that would sway you from your commitment to your personal moral compass. It is also good to use in situations in which you are defending yourself against harassment or criminal incursions, such as break-ins or theft. It can also help you maintain your confidence in a chaotic situation.

OTHALA

The rune of inheritance, estate, and family, Othala is the rune to use when working to protect your house and home. Family involves ancestors, which means you can draw on their power and energy when working to protect family members and your home as well as your possessions.

BIND RUNES

The use of bind runes is probably as old as the use of runes themselves. A bind rune is formed when two or more runes are laid on top of one another along a shared axis or stroke to form a single symbol. This also combines the energies expressed by each rune. For example, combining Algiz and Raidho creates a rune for safe travel.

CIRCLE

A circle is a very simple shape, but it has many positive associations. A circle has no corners in which negative energy can gather. A circle can serve as a barrier, holding something inside safely or preventing incursion by attack. It also symbolizes unity.

HEX SIGNS

Pennsylvania Dutch hex signs, hung or painted on the exterior of houses and barns, date from the mid-nineteenth century in Pennsylvania's south Lancaster County. They are said to be based on traditional folk art, but there's an underlying energy to the symbols used, which tend to be protection symbols or symbols that attract or repel certain energies. Early examples were stars in circles, both protection symbols; the stars have five, six, or eight points.